AN ILLUSTRATED DATA GUIDE TO

MODERN RECONNAISSANCE AIRCRAFT

Compiled by
Christopher Chant

TIGER BOOKS INTERNATIONAL
LONDON

This edition published in 1997 by
Tiger Books International PLC
Twickenham

Published in Canada in 1997 by
Vanwell Publishing Limited
St. Catharines, Ontario

© Graham Beehag Books
Christchurch
Dorset

Printed in Hong Kong

ISBN 1-85501-864-0

CONTENTS

Boeing E-3 **S**entry

Manufacturer: Boeing Military Airplanes Division of Boeing Defense & Space Group within the Boeing Company

Country of origin: USA

Specification: E-3C Sentry

Type: AWACS (airborne warning and control system) platform

Accommodation: Flightcrew of four, and a mission crew of 16 carried in the cabin

Entered service: January 1979

Left service: Still in service

Operational equipment: Standard communication and navigation equipment, plus IBM 4 Pi CC-1 high-speed computer, Westinghouse APY-2 (upgraded APY-1) surveillance radar and AIL APX-103 IFF/TADIL-J (tactical digital information link - joint) system, Sanders Improved Self-Defense System IR jammer, nine Hazeltine multi-purpose and two auxiliary display consoles, and Bendix APS-133 weather/mapping radar, two Delco ASN-119 Carousel IV INSs updated by Northrop ARN-120 Omega, Teledyne Ryan APN-213 Doppler navigation and GPS

Powerplant: Four Pratt & Whitney TF33-P-100/100A turbofans each rated at 21,000lb st (93.41kN) dry

Fuel capacity: Internal fuel 19,973.7 Imp gal (90,800.4 litres); external fuel none; provision for inflight refuelling

Dimensions: Span 145ft 9in (44.42m); aspect ratio 6.96; area 3,050.00sq ft (283.35sq m); length 152ft 11in (46.61m); height 41ft 9in (12.73m); tailplane span 45ft 9in (13.94m); wheel track 22ft 1in (6.73m); wheelbase 59ft 0in (17.98m)

Weights: Empty 171,950lb (77,996kg) operating; normal

With its powerful surveillance radar and massive onboard computing capability, the E-3 Sentry is a potent 'force multiplier' essential to the success of USAF operations.

take-off 325,000lb (147,420kg); maximum take-off 332,500lb (150,822kg)

Performance: Maximum level speed 'clean' 460kt (530mph; 853km/h) at high altitude; cruising speed, maximum 443kt (510mph; 821km/h) at 29,000ft 8,840m); radius 870nm (1,002 miles; 1,612km) for a patrol of 6hr 0min without inflight refuelling; endurance more than 11hr 0min without inflight refuelling; service ceiling 29,000ft (8,840m) with the radar operational

Variants
EC-137C: One of the most expensive but important aircraft types in the current military inventory, the E-3 Sentry is a highly capable AWACS platform designed for three-dimensional surveillance of a massive volume of airspace and the direction of aerial operations within that volume. The importance of such aircraft began to emerge late in World War II (1939-45), especially in the context of naval operations otherwise reliant on the short electromagnetic horizon of shipborne radars, and the US Navy expended considerable and successful effort on the development of aerial 'radar pickets' such as the

carrierborne Grumman WF (later E-1) Tracer and land-based Lockheed WV (later EC-121) Warning Star that was also operated by the US Air Force (USAF). Apart from the relatively primitive nature of the types' radar (the Warning Star had to carry separate azimuth- and height-finding radars below and above the fuselage respectively), the principal limitation of these types was the relatively low cruising ceiling imposed by their piston-engined powerplants.

In planning a successor to the Warning Star, the USAF decided that turbine propulsion was a necessity as it would provide a cruising ceiling of some 30,000ft (9,144m) for a radar horizon of 215nm (248 miles; 399km) compared with the Warning Star's radar horizon of 130nm (150 miles; 241km) from its cruising altitude of 20,000ft (6,096m). The USAF also determined that a new generation of radar was needed, as existing equipments lacked effective look-down capability. The lack of such a radar had been no real limitation in the 1950s, for bombers and other attack warplanes had to operate at high altitude to secure worthwhile range with their fuel-thirsty turbojet engines, but low-level penetration and attack were becoming the operational norms in the 1960s as the threat of SAMs increased and fuel-economical turbofan engines became common.

In 1965, therefore, the USAF communications system, and limited overwater sensor capability. The first upgraded machine re-entered service in July 1984.

E-3C Sentry: This is the standard to which the nine Standard E-3As were upgraded between 1980 and 1983, with the APY-2 radar for full overwater and overland capability, five extra situation display consoles (as in the E-3B), additional UHF radio gear and the 'Have Quick-A' communications system. The type can also be fitted with small underwing pylons for the AIM-9 Sidewinder short-range AAMs that can, in theory, provide this immensely important and costly 'force multiplier' type with a modest self-defence capability.

While the E-3 is a derivative of the Model 707 airliner, the E-4 is a derivative of the larger Model 747 'jumbo jet', and serves in small numbers as a survivable national airborne command-post type for the long-endurance carriage of the US president and other high-ranking officials in the event of nuclear war.

E-3D Sentry: This designation is applied to the seven aircraft delivered to the RAF. They are basically similar to the NATO aircraft but have a powerplant of four CFM56-2A-2 turbofans, each rated at 22,000lb st (97.86kN) dry and supplied with fuel from an internal weight of 155,448lb (70,511kg), for a service ceiling of more than 30,000ft (9,144m). The variant also carries the MEL ARI.18240/1 'Orange Gate' (license-built Loral EW-1017) ESM system in wingtip pods that increase the span to 147ft 7in (44.98m), and the radar is modified for overwater use. The aircraft were delivered from 1990 with the designation Sentry AEW.Mk 1, and have provision for inflight refuelling using the flying boom or HDU systems, the latter made possible by the installation of a probe above the flightdeck.

E-3F Sentry: These four aircraft are basically similar to the E-3D but were delivered between May 1991 and February 1992 to the French air force, and are thus fitted with the Link 11 and 16 data-links associated with the French STRIDA defence network.

E-6A Mercury: First flown in February 1987 for a service debut in August 1989, these 16 US Navy aircraft are based on the airframe of the Advanced Model 707-320 but powered by four CFM International F108-CF-100 (CFM56-2A-2) turbofans each rated at 22,000lb st (97.86kN) dry and supplied with fuel from an internal weight of 155,000lb (70,308kg). The type incorporates the special electronics (USC-14 communications centre and USC-13 transmit/receive gear including ARC-182 VLF radio) to provide a communication relay facility between command-post aircraft and submerged missile-armed nuclear submarines.

This is the TACAMO (take charge and move out) concept, and the E-6A is the TACAMO II type replacing the Lockheed EC-130Q TACAMO I. The TACAMO II system uses the ARC-182 radio transmitting through a dipole aerial system that employs single long and short trailing wire aerials of some 26,000 and 4,000ft (7,925 and 1,219m) respectively: these are deployed from their stowed positions under the rear cabin and under the tailplane leading edge as the E-6A patrols at an altitude between 25,000 and 30,000ft (7,620 and 9,144m). Other electronic items include the General Instruments ALR-66(V)4 ESM equipment carried in the starboard wingtip pod; the avionics include an accurate long-range Litton INS based on three LTN-90 ring-laser platforms integrated with a Litton LTN-211 Omega, and the electronics are hardened against electromagnetic pulse effects.

The E-6A has a flightcrew of four and a mission crew of six, with another eight seats available for relief crew, and its data include a span of 148ft 2in (45.16m) with an aspect ratio of 7.20 and an area of 3,050.00sq ft (283.35sq m); operating empty weight of 172,795lb (78,380kg); maximum take-off weight of 342,000lb (155,131kg); dash speed of 530kt (610mph; 981km/h) at optimum altitude; maximum cruising speed of 455kt (524mph; 843km/h) at 40,000ft (12,191m); mission range of 6,350nm (7,307 miles; 11,759km) without inflight refuelling; radius of 1,000nm (1,152 miles; 1,854km) for a patrol of 10hr 30min without inflight refuelling, or of 28hr 54min with one inflight refuelling, or of 72hr with multiple inflight refuellings before the point of crew exhaustion is reached; endurance of 15hr 24min with inflight refuelling; service ceiling of 42,000ft (12,801m), and patrol altitude between 25,000 and 30,000ft (7,620 and 9,144m).

E-8A: First flown in December 1988, this initial variant of the C-18 military version of the Advanced Model 707-300 was planned and developed as the E-18C but has since been redesignated E-8A as a battlefield surveillance and targeting aircraft with the JSTARS (joint surveillance and target attack reconnaissance system, later joint surveillance and target acquisition radar system) equipment in a combined USAF and US Army effort.

The two E-A aircraft were designed to validate the JSTARS concept (fully vindicated in the 1991 UN-led war to drive Iraqi invaders out of Kuwait) and the technical programme which is being run by Boeing, with Grumman responsible for the mission equipment. This equipment is centred on the all-important SLAR, which is a Norden phased-array multi-mode equipment operating in synthetic-aperture mode for surveillance of stationary targets such as artillery in firing position, and in Doppler mode for the surveillance of slow-moving targets such as armoured forces on the march. The SLAR's antenna is located in a 'canoe' fairing some 24ft 0in (7.32m) long under the forward fuselage, and the radar has a range of 140nm (161 miles; 259km) as it alternates between synthetic-aperture and pulse-Doppler modes. Radar data are fed to 10 large-screen graphics consoles, and are then transmitted via the JTIDS to relevant fighters and/or Motorola TSQ-132S-280 ground-station modules.

The E-8A has a flight crew of four and a mission crew of some 21 or 34 for standard- or long-endurance missions, and at a maximum take-off weight of 333,600lb (151,320kg) has a cruising speed of 525kt (605mph; 973km/h) at 25,000ft (7,620m) on the power of its four Pratt & Whitney JT3D-7 turbofans, each rated at 19,000lb st (84.51kN) dry and supplied with fuel from an internal weight of 159,560lb (72,376kg) for a maximum range of 5,000nm (5,758 miles; 9,265km).

E-8C: It had been planned to produce the JSTARS type as the E-8B using new-build airframes powered by four CFM International F108 (CFM56) turbofans each rated at 22,000lb st (97.86kN) dry, but this scheme was overtaken by Boeing's closure of its Model 707 production line.

The JSTARS 'production' version will thus be the E-8C using ex-airline Advanced Model 707-300s completely refurbished and fitted with an updated version of the

JSTARS equipment with 18 graphics consoles including one tasked solely with defensive (warning) work. The first five of a planned 21 aircraft were ordered in 1992 for delivery from 1995 in anticipation of full service from 1997.

IAI Model 707 Phalcon: Developed by Israel Aircraft Industries, this is a Model 707 airborne early warning (AEW) conversion with the Elta EL/2075 Phalcon electronically steered phased-array radar, which at a patrol altitude of 30,000ft (9,144m) can detect warships and fighter-sized aerial targets at a range of 216nm (249 miles; 400km) and helicopter-sized aerial targets at a range of 97nm (112 miles; 180km). The advantage of this electronically-steered radar over the type using a rotating antenna (as in the Boeing E-3 Sentry and Northrop Grumman E-2 Hawkeye) includes a reduction in target-recognition time from some 12 seconds to between 2 and 4 seconds.

The radar is a modular system that can be configured for an optional number of antenna arrays, the current standard being three arrays (two on the sides of the forward fuselage in cheek positions, and one in the nose under a large radome that does not interfere with the pilots' fields of vision); the drag of the antennae has only a marginal effect on overall performance, which includes a typical mission endurance of between 8 and 10 hours. The configuration of the three antennae provides surveillance through 260 degrees in azimuth, and can be increased to 360 degrees by the addition of more antenna arrays.

The Phalcon is more than just an AEW type, moreover, for it includes Elta ESM and Comint systems. The ESM system uses four antennae (one each at the nose, tail and wingtips) and provides Elint as well as tactical ESM capability, while the Comint system is based on the highly capable EL/K-7031 receiver suite. The erstwhile cabin is laid out with 13 work stations (nos 1 and 2 for test equipment operators, nos 3 and 4 for radar system managers, nos 5 and 6 for Elint and ESM operators, no. 7 for the mission commander, nos 8, 9 and 10 for the radar operators, no. 11 for the communications support operator, and nos 12 and 13 for the data-link management and communications operators).

The first Phalcon was delivered to Chile in 1993.

Ilyushin A-50 'Mainstay'

Manufacturer: Aviation Complex 'S.V. Ilyushin' (originally Ilyushin Design Bureau) with further development by the Taganrog Aviation Scientific-Technical Complex 'G.M. Beriev' (originally Beriev Design Bureau)

Country of origin: CIS (originally USSR)

Specification: A-50U 'Mainstay'

Type: AWACS (airborne warning and control system) aeroplane

Accommodation: Flight and mission crew of 15

Entered service: (Il-76 series) 1976

Left service: Still in service

Operational equipment: Standard communication and navigation equipment, weather and mapping radar, plus automatic flight-control system, Vega Schmel-M surveillance and tracking radar, RWR, ECM and packs of 96 flares fitted in the landing gear fairings and/or rear fuselage sides

Powerplant: Four PNPP 'Aviadvigatel' (Soloviev) D-30KP turbofans each rated at 26,455lb st (117.68kN) dry

Fuel capacity: Internal fuel about 18,000 Imp gal (81,830 litres); external fuel none; provision for inflight refuelling

Dimensions: Span 165ft 8in (50.50m); aspect ratio 8.50; area 3,229.28sq ft (300.00sq m); length more than 152ft 10.25in (46.59m); height 48ft 5in (14.76m)

Weights: Maximum take-off 374,780lb (170,000kg)

Performance: Maximum level speed 'clean' 459kt (528mph; 850km/h) at optimum altitude; cruising speed, maximum 432kt (497mph; 800km/h) between 29,530 and 39,370ft (9,000 and 12,000m) and economical between 405kt (466mph; 750km/h) between 29,530 and 39,370ft (9,000 and 12,000m); ferry range 3,617nm (4,163 miles; 6,698km); service ceiling about 47,570ft (14,500m)

Variants
A-50 'Mainstay': First flown in prototype form during March 1971, the Ilyushin Il-76 'Candid' was designed as the Soviet replacement for the Antonov An-12 'Cub' series in both the civil freighting and military transport roles, with a powerplant of four PNPP 'Aviadvigatel' (Soloviev) D-30KP turbofans. Design of the new type began in the late 1960s to meet a requirement for a freighter able to carry a payload of 88,183lb (40,000kg) over a range of 2,698nm (3,107 miles; 5,000km) in less than 6 hours, able to operate from short and unprepared airstrips, and capable of coping with the worst weather conditions likely to be

experienced in Siberia and the USSR's arctic regions.

The configuration of the new Soviet transport was probably inspired by that of an American logistic freighter, the Lockheed C-141A StarLifter, in its overall layout with a circular-section fuselage offering pressurised accommodation, swept flying surfaces including a high-set wing and T-tail, a powerplant of four fuel-economical turbofans pod-mounted below and ahead of the wings, and multi-wheel landing gear of the tricycle type, in this instance with a nose unit carrying two side-by-side pairs of wheels and the main units (retracting into two ventral/lateral blisters whose use left the fuselage clear for payload) each comprising a tandem arrangement of two four-wheel axles.

One of the major keys to the type's success as an airlifter, as in any modern type fulfilling the same role, is the design of the upswept rear fuselage that allowed the incorporation of a ventral ramp/door arrangement for uncomplicated loading and unloading of bulky items as well as the paradropping of heavy equipment and/or personnel. In the case of the Il-76, the ramp/door arrangement is hydraulically powered and comprises two outward-hinging clamshell doors, a downward-hinging ramp, and an upward-and inward-hinging panel between the clamshell doors. This arrangement provides unobstructed access to the rect-angular-section hold, which is 65ft 7in (20.00m) long or 80ft

The type replaced by the Ilyushin A-50 'Mainstay' was the Tupolev Tu-126 'Moss', which was a highly limited AWACS platform by comparison with the Boeing E-3 Sentry.

5in (24.50m) including the ramp, 11ft 4in (3.46m) wide and 11ft 2in (3.40m) high. The hold can handle freight with the aid of roller panels in the floor and two overhead cranes, each carrying one hoist rated at 6,614lb (3,000kg) or two hoists each rated at 5,511lb (2,500kg).

The Il-76 has been produced in subvariants for the civil and military roles, the latter being readily identifiable by their manned rear gun turrets carrying two 23mm Gryazev-Shipunov GSh-23 cannon. The four primary military variants are the basic Il-76 'Candid-A' with a powerplant of four D-30KP turbofans; the Il-76M 'Candid-B' based on the improved Il-76T model with 22,046lb (10,000kg) of additional fuel in a centre-section tank above a hold that can carry 125 paratroops or 140 troops as an alternative to freight, a rear turret, ECM blisters on the fuselage sides in line with the navigator's compartment, and provision for chaff/flare dispenser packs; the Il-76MD 'Candid-B' military subvariant equivalent to the civil Il-76TD with more fuel and D-30KP-2 turbofans able to maintain their power up to higher altitudes and ambient temperatures for the carriage of a maximum payload of 105,820lb (48,000kg) at a maximum take-off weight of 418,871lb (190,000kg); and the Il-76MF 'Candid-?' with the hold lengthened by 21ft 8in (6.60m) for the carriage of a maximum payload of 114,640lb (52,000kg) on a powerplant of four 'Aviadvigatel' PS-90AN turbofans each rated at 35,275lb st (156.86kN).

All these variants are extremely capable, their combination of advanced design, sturdy landing gear, excellent high-lift devices (slats over the full leading-edge span and triple-slotted flaps over 75 per cent of the trailing-edge span), and powerful engines bestowing good field performance even under adverse conditions.

Entering service in 1984, the A-50 'Mainstay' is the AEW version of the Il-76 freighter developed from the mid-1970s to replace the Tupolev Tu-126 'Moss'. The type has a lengthened forward fuselage providing the additional volume required for the tactical compartment in which the mission personnel of the 15-man crew derive data from the large Liana surveillance radar with its antenna in an over-fuselage rotodome, which has a diameter of 29ft 9in (9.00m).

Other changes include deletion of the tail turret, addition of a satellite navigation and communications system, installation of comprehensive IFF equipment, and fitting of active/passive EW systems including an ESM system with some of its antennae in the tail. The transport model's glazed nose is replaced by a unit with a single transparency on each side, the forward fuselage in front of the wing centre-section supports a large 'canoe' fairing over what is probably the antenna for the A-50's satellite navigation and communications system, the port main landing gear blister carries a horizontal winglet, a large ram-air scoop is fitted in the base of the fin to provide cooling

The fleet of reconnaissance and electronic warfare aircraft fielded by the USSR (now the CIS) was boosted from the mid-1980s by several conversions of obsolescent Ilyushin Il-18 civil transports as Il-20 'Coot-A' Elint and Il-22 'Coot-B' airborne command-post aircraft, the former with specialised intelligence-gathering equipment and the latter with dedicated command and communication equipment.

air for the mass of new electronic equipment, and an inflight-refuelling probe is fitted.

Full production at the rate of five aircraft per year was drastically slowed in 1990, probably as a result of the severe economic problems encountered by the CIS from that time, but the current force has allowed the Tu-126 to be phased out or at least relegated to secondary areas. It is worth noting that weight constraints prevent the A-50 from taking-off with a full fuel load and, as inflight refuelling is difficult because of aerodynamic problems, endurance is lower than anticipated. In addition, it is likely that crew performance is degraded by the A-50's lack of rest facilities.

The latest version is the A-50U 'Mainstay' with the advanced Vega Shmel-M radar that is claimed to offer parity with the APY-2 radar of the Boeing E-3C Sentry. This is a 3D pulse-Doppler radar able to detect fighter-sized air targets at a range of 124nm (143 miles; 230km) or a ship at a range of 216nm (249 miles; 400km). The mission crew of 10 can track 50 separate targets simultaneously and control up to 10 simultaneous interceptions.

Adnan 1: In 1989 Iraq revealed that it had undertaken initial development of the Baghdad 1 AEW platform, based on the Il-76MD with its rear ramp/door replaced by a glassfibre-reinforced plastic radome over the antenna of the Thomson-CSF Tiger G surveillance radar (supplied by France), to produce a system providing coverage through more than 180 degrees but less than 360 degrees. Developed in parallel was a more orthodox AEW platform based on the same airframe, and this Adnan 1 then replaced the Baghdad 1 in Iraqi plans. The Adnan 1 has its radar antenna located in an over-fuselage rotodome to provide coverage through 360 degrees.

Radar developments were introduced to reduce the problem of ground clutter, and the system's claimed performance included the detection, tracking and identification of targets to a maximum range of 189nm (217.5 miles; 350km), these data being passed by the four-man mission crew to a ground station by voice or data-link. The Adnan 1 also possessed ESM systems and a Cossor IFF system.

Adnan 2: Under this designation Iraq was upgrading the Adnan 1 concept with a control function to allow the direct vectoring of fighter aircraft. The status of the programme is uncertain in the aftermath of Iraq's defeat in 1991.

Lockheed Martin EC-130 Hercules

Manufacturer: Lockheed Martin Aeronautical Systems (originally Lockheed-Georgia Company, and later Lockheed Aeronautical Systems Company of the Lockheed Aircraft Corporation)

Country of origin: USA

Specification: EC-130E Hercules

Type: Airborne battlefield command and control centre (ABCCC)

Accommodation: Flightcrew of four or five, and a mission crew of up to 12

Entered service: (C-130 series) December 1956

Left service: Still in service

Still the tactical transport workhorse of many of the world's air forces, the Lockheed Martin C-130 Hercules has gone through four main variants in its basic form, and each of these has spawned a number of variants for more specialised roles.

Operational equipment: Standard communication and navigation equipment, plus Texas Instruments APQ-122(V)1 weather/mapping radar, Litton ALR-69 RWR and Sanders ALQ-156 missile-detection system (being replaced by AAR-47 missile warning and countermeasures implementation system, ALE-47 chaff/flare dispenser and ALQ-157 IR countermeasures system)

Powerplant: Four Allison T56-A-17 turboprops each rated at 4,050ehp (3,020ekW) for take-off

Fuel capacity: Internal fuel 5,417.5 Imp gal (24,627.8 litres) increased to 5,795.5 Imp gal (26,346.4 litres) from the 359th machine onwards, plus provision for 2,264.9 Imp gal (10,296.3 litres) in two 1,132.5 Imp gal (5,148.1 litre) underwing tanks; provision for inflight refuelling

Dimensions: Span 132ft 7in (40.41m); aspect ratio 10.09; area 1,745.00sq ft (162.12sq m); length 97ft 9in (29.79m); height 38ft 3in (11.66m); tailplane span 52ft 8in (16.05m); wheel track 14ft 3in (4.35m); wheelbase 32ft 0.75in (9.77m)

Weights: Empty 72,892lb (33,063kg) operating

Performance: Maximum level speed 'clean' 330kt

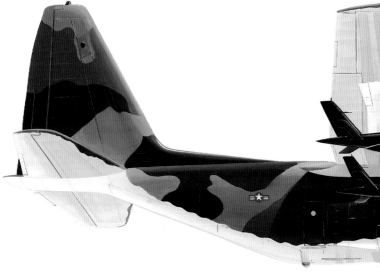

(380mph; 612km/h) at 30,000ft (9,144m); cruising speed, maximum 320kt (368mph; 592km/h) at optimum altitude; range 4,082nm (4,700 miles; 7,564km) with a payload of 45,000lb (20,412kg); maximum rate of climb at sea level 1,830ft (558m) per minute; service ceiling 33,000ft (10,058m)

Variants
C-130A-II Hercules: Now a product of the Lockheed Martin Corporation since the 1994 merger of the Lockheed Corporation and Martin Marietta, the Hercules is a classic airlifter, and as such is the mainstay of the tactical air transport capability possessed by many Western air arms. The type has its origins in the early 1950s, yet is still in full production and development. From the time it became embroiled in the Korean War (1950-53) the USAF found that its Fairchild C-119 Flying Boxcar tactical transport, which had only just entered service at that time, lacked adequate performance and payload. In February 1951, therefore, the USAF issued a far-sighted tactical airlifter requirement to Boeing, Douglas, Fairchild and Lockheed. The requirement called for an aeroplane able to carry 92 infantrymen or 64 paratroops over a radius of 1,100nm (1,267 miles; 2,039km) or a freight payload of 30,000lb (13,608kg) over a radius of 950nm (1,093 miles; 1,759km), the provision of two side doors for minimum-dispersal paratroop drops as well as an integral rear ramp/door arrangement openable in flight, the capability to operate from short and/or unprepared airstrips, and the ability to fly at speeds down to 125kt (144mph; 232km/h) in paradropping operations (or even lower for assault landings).

In July 1951 the Lockheed Model 82 was declared winner of the design competition, securing an order for two YC-130 prototypes. The company's objective had been to exceed the USAF's requirement wherever possible, and the core of its design was a hold of nearly square section with the length to accommodate a sizeable payload comprising a whole range of tactical equipment in a volume of 4,500cu ft (127.43cu m). The hold was 41ft 5in (12.60m) long with the ramp raised and 51ft 8.5in (15.76m) long with the ramp lowered, 10ft 3in (3.12m) wide and 9ft 2.75in (2.81m) high, and was fitted with a large upward-hinging freight door on the port side, just behind the crew door leading to the flightdeck. The hold was

located around the machine's centre of gravity. The flattened circular-section fuselage accommodated the five-man flightdeck in the nose, then the hold, and at the tail an upswept empennage above the hydraulically powered ventral ramp/door arrangement that provided unobstructed access to the hold and could also be opened in flight for the delivery of air-dropped loads. The hold's floor was placed at truckbed height to facilitate loading and unloading, and this required short legs for the tricycle landing gear, which comprised a two-wheel forward unit retracting into the lower nose and tandem main units on each side retracting into external fairings that left the hold unobstructed; all the tyres were of the low-pressure type.

The powerplant was located on the wing, which was placed in the high-set position to provide the propellers with adequate ground clearance, and whereas the obvious choice for a tactical airlifter was two potent and well-proved engines (either piston engines or turboprops), the design team selected four powerful but comparatively immature turboprops for a combination of good reliability and the capability for the adoption of higher-powered engines as heavier versions of the airlifter were introduced.

The first YC-130 was used initially for static tests, and the type's initial flight was made in August 1954 by the second YC-130 with a powerplant of four Allison T56-A-1 turboprops each rated at 3,250ehp (2,423ekW) and driving a three-blade propeller. The USAF had meanwhile ordered

Seen here in the form of a standard transport of the Italian air force, the C-130H is the last of the original series of Hercules aircraft to be produced before the advent of the wholly modernised C-130J in the later 1990s, and has also been adapted for a number of specialised reconnaissance and electronic warfare roles.

the Model 182 derivative into production as the C-130A Hercules, and the first of these aircraft flew in April 1955 with a powerplant of four T56-A-1A turboprops each rated at 3,750ehp (2,796ekW), replaced from the 51st machine by T56-A-9 or -11 turboprops of identical rating but still supplied with fuel from the same internal capacity of 4,205.1 Imp gal (19,116.3 litres). The other main changes were provision for two 416.3 Imp gal (1,892.7 litre) auxiliary tanks in the fuselage, although this facility was soon replaced by provision for two 374.7 Imp gal (1,703.4 litre) non-jettisonable tanks under the outer wing panels. The aircraft were delivered with three-blade Aeroproducts propellers, but in 1978 were revised with the four-blade Hamilton Standard propellers that became standard on the C-130B.

The first of 207 C-130A transports was delivered in October 1956 for service from December of the same year, and the designation C-130A-II was applied to C-130A transports converted for the combined Comint/Sigint role with receivers, direction finders, signal analysers, pulse analysers, recorders, and a hold-accommodated mission

The EC-130E is characterised by large but narrow antennae under the wings, outboard of the engines but inboard of the two pods which can deploy trailing wire antennae for very-low-frequency communications capability.

crew of between 12 and 15 operators. The aircraft were based in Europe; one of the machines was shot down over Armenia in September 1958, and the surviving aircraft were later returned to basic C-130A standard.

C-130B-II Hercules: The C-130B (Model 282) improved second-generation version of the Hercules airlifter was made possible by the availability of the more potent T56-A-7 or -7A turboprop rated at 4,050ehp (3,020ekW) and driving a four-blade propeller, in the same four-engined powerplant supplied with fuel from an internal capacity increased to 5,795.5 Imp gal (26,346.4 litres) to allow the removal of the drag-inducing underwing tanks. The first of an eventual 133 examples of the C-130B series was delivered from December 1958 and entered USAF service in June 1959, subsequently paving the way for a number of more specialised derivatives including the C-130B-II Hercules (later designated the RC-130B Hercules), of which 13 were converted from C-130B standard for the 'Sun Valley II' Comint/Sigint role with an updated version of the C-130A-II's mission suite.

EC-130E Hercules: The C-130E third production variant of the basic transport was evolved as the Model 382 to meet the demands of both the Tactical Air Command (TAC) for additional tactical transports and the Military Air Transport Service (MATS) for a logistic transport offering better payload/range performance than its current force of piston-engined medium transports. In essence, the C-130E was a long-range version of the C-130B with an increased internal fuel capacity plus provision for two underwing tanks relocated from the C-130's positions under the outer wing panels to attachments between the engine nacelles. Other changes were stronger wing spars, thicker skin panels and strengthened landing gear units.

The first of an eventual 390 examples of the C-130E series for the US forces flew in August 1961 for delivery from April 1962. Production of the basic C-130E totalled 109 export aircraft and 377 aircraft for the USAF (255 TAC and 122 MATS machines all pooled under control of the Military Airlift Command from 1974-75), and the USAF has also operated its aircraft in a number of converted subvariants including the EC-130E, which was a designation applied to five groups of aircraft of which only three could be differentiated by their designations. The two types that operated under the plain EC-130E designation included one machine delivered to the US Coast Guard for the world-wide calibration of LORAN (long-range air navigation) equipment, and at least three aircraft operated by the USAF for classified Elint, Sigint and/or Comint work in Europe.

The three groups differentiated in their designations were the EC-130E(ABCCC), EC-130E 'Comfy Levi' and EC-130E 'Rivet Rider'.

Originally designated C-130E-II Hercules up to April 1977, the EC-130E(ABCCC) was developed during the Vietnam War as an airborne battlefield command and control centre ABCCC to control air attacks on the basis of data from forward air controllers, flareships, ground observers, ground sensors and several types of reconnaissance. The core of this command capability is the insertion into the hold of the Unisys ASC-15 ABCCC III command battle staff module, with accommodation for between 12 and 16 operators and command staff personnel as well as advanced communications equipment. The model can be distinguished from standard C-130Es by its additional antennae (including two large forward-facing HF probes under the outer wing panels) and the provision of a ram-air inlet on each side of the forward fuselage to cool the ASC-15's electronic equipment. At least eight aircraft were converted to this standard, and four of them were later updated to C-130H standard with an inflight-refuelling receptacle and T56-A-15 turboprops, but the frequently quoted EC-130H(ABCCC) designation has not been applied.

The EC-130E 'Comfy Levi' designation was applied to

five aircraft converted for a highly classified Elint and jammer role with just a few additional antennae to distinguish it from the standard C-130E, and four of the aircraft were later upgraded to a partial C-130H standard with an inflight-refuelling receptacle and T56-A-15 engines.

The EC-130E 'Rivet Rider' designation is applied to four aircraft converted for the emergency broadcast (TV and radio) role in the event of a national emergency. The type has three pods (one under the tail and one under each wingtip) for trailing wire antennae, and three large blade antennae (one in the dorsal fin position and the other two under the outer wing panels), and a heat exchanger on each side of the rear fuselage to dissipate the heat of the additional mission equipment, which is located in the hold together with a complement of between seven and 13 specialists. The aircraft have a higher empty weight than any other Hercules variant, and therefore suffer in performance terms even after the partial upgrade to C-130H standard with an inflight-refuelling receptacle and T56-A-15 turboprops. The aircraft are being updated with colour rather than black-and-white TV transmission capability.

EC-130G Hercules: The C-130G is the US Navy equivalent of the C-130E, and differs in its powerplant of four T56-A-16 turboprops each rated at 4,910ehp (3,661ekW). The four aircraft were initially used as transports, but were then revised to EC-130G standard to provide a communications link between the US national command authority and submerged nuclear-powered ballistic missile submarines. For this vital role the main change was the installation of the TACAMO II package, based on a VLF/UHF radio installation using two very long trailing wire antennae streamed from tubes in the rear ramp and under the tail unit.

This model differed from the C-130F in its powerplant of four T56-A-7A turboprops each rated at 4,050ehp (3,020ekW), internal fuel capacity of 5,795 Imp gal (26,346 litres) supplemented by 2,265 Imp gal (10,296 litres) in two underwing tanks, normal take-off weight of 155,000lb (70,308kg) and maximum take-off weight of 175,000lb (79,380kg). With the TACAMO role now undertaken by the Boeing E-6A Hermes, three of the four surplus EC-130Gs may be converted to TC-130G Hercules crew trainer-/utility standard.

EC-130H Hercules: Developed in the early 1960s for the export market, and first delivered in March 1965 in the form of a machine for the Royal New Zealand air force, the C-130H is the current production standard of the Hercules family but is about to be supplanted by the improved C-160J Hercules with a 'glass' cockpit, new-generation engines driving more-advanced propellers, and a thoroughly revitalised and modernised airframe.

The C-130H is basically an improved version of the C-130E with a powerplant of four T56-A-15 turboprops each rated at 4,910ehp (3,661ekW) but normally derated to 4,508ehp (3,362ekW), and a number of enhancements in the airframe and avionics. The airframe modifications include a strengthened wing centre-section box and a better braking system, while the avionics modifications include an INS, Omega navigation, and provision for RDR-1F or APS-13 radar in place of the original APN-59B and APQ-122 radars.

The C-130H has become the major production model, built in larger numbers than any other variant and still in production during the mid-1990s, and has inevitably spawned a large number of special-purpose subvariants including the EC-130H, of which four were produced as conversions for the 'Compass Call II' communications jamming role with a special equipment package installed in the hold. The type has a distinctive appearance as a result of the trestle-type antenna array under the tailplane and on each side of the vertical tail surface, two blister fairings on the sides of the rear fuselage, and ram-air inlets at the front of the landing gear fairings. The EC-130H has a maximum payload of 45,000lb (20,412kg) and a basic empty weight of 72,892lb (33,063kg).

EC-130Q Hercules: This was an advanced version of the EC-130G for the TACAMO role associated with communications relay between the national command authority and submerged SSBNs. Some 18 aircraft were built with a powerplant of four T56-A-16 turboprops each rated at 4,910ehp (3,661ekW), the TACAMO III, IV or IVB equipment suites including a 26,000ft (7,925m) aerial streamed from the position under the tail and a 5,000ft (1,524m) aerial streamed from the position in the ramp, and ESM in two wingtip pods. The aircraft were retired in 1992, and while 14 were placed in storage, two were passed to NASA and two were stripped of their TACAMO suites to become TC-130Q crew trainer/transport aircraft.

Lockheed Martin SR-71

Manufacturer: Lockheed Martin 'Skunk Works' of the Lockheed Martin Corporation (originally Lockheed-California Company and later Lockheed Aeronautical Systems Company of the Lockheed Aircraft Corporation)

Country of origin: USA

Specification: SR-71A 'Blackbird'

Type: Strategic reconnaissance aeroplane

Accommodation: Pilot and reconnaissance systems operator in tandem on Lockheed zero/zero ejector seats

Entered service: About 1963

Left service: Still in service

Operational equipment: Standard communication and navigation equipment, plus a large number of classified optical, optronic, thermal and electronic reconnaissance systems, and ECM

Powerplant: Two Pratt & Whitney JT11D-20B bleed turbojets each rated at 23,000lb st (102.31kN) dry and 32,500lb st (144.57kN) with afterburning

Fuel capacity: Internal fuel 84,180lb (38,184kg); external fuel none; provision for inflight refuelling

Dimensions: Span 55ft 7in (16.94m); aspect ratio 1.72; area 1,800.00sq ft (167.22sq m); length 103ft 10in (31.66m) excluding pitot boom and 107ft 5in (32.74m) including pitot boom; height 18ft 6in (5.64m); wheel track 17ft 0in (5.18m); wheelbase 34ft 0in (10.36m)

Weights: Empty 60,000lb (27,216kg); normal take-off 145,000lb (65,772kg); maximum take-off 170,000lb (77,112kg)

In its time one of the most advanced aircraft in the world in terms of its airframe and powerplant, and still the holder of the world absolute speed and sustained altitude records, the Lockheed Martin SR-71A now survives only in very small numbers after the USAF tried to eliminate its whole fleet on the grounds of high cost and limited reconnaissance capability. The type is nicknamed 'Blackbird' as a result of its overall finish in a black material that helps in the dissipation of heat during high-speed flight.

Performance: Maximum level speed 'clean' 2,005kt (2,309mph; 3,715km/h) or Mach 3.5 at high altitude; cruising speed, maximum 1,720kt (1,981 mph; 3,187km/h) or Mach 3 at high altitude; range 2,600nm (2,994 miles; 4,818km); radius typically 1,050nm (1,209 miles; 1,946km); endurance 1hr 30min at high altitude without inflight refuelling; service ceiling 100,000ft (30,480m)

Variants
A-12: Retired from service in the early 1990s but then restored to operational capability in limited numbers (just three aircraft) during the middle of the decade, the SR-71A is the world's supreme strategic reconnaissance platform, and offers unrivalled capabilities in the performance of reconnaissance duties at extremely high altitudes and at very high speeds: indeed, this extraordinary machine is still

the official holder of the world absolute speed and altitude records. The origins of the SR-71 concept can be traced back to 1954 when a British engineer working for the Summers Gyroscope Company of Santa Monica, California, submitted to the USAF's Air Research and Development Command an unsolicited proposal for a high-altitude aeroplane powered by a three-stage turboprop running on liquid oxygen and liquid hydrogen. The USAF was sufficiently interested, and in October 1955 placed a contract with the Garrett AiResearch Corporation (which had recently bought Summers' liquid-hydrogen engine interests) for concept definition of three such engines (the Rex I and II turboprops, and the Rex III turbojet) and aircraft to be powered by them.

Garrett subcontracted the airframe portion of its contracts to Lockheed during November 1955, and the first result was the Lockheed CL-325-1 design for a machine able to reach 1,435kt (1,653mph; 2,660km/h) or Mach 2.5 at 100,000ft (30,480m) on the power of two Rex III engines in a straight-winged airframe notable for its span of 79ft 10.5in (24.35m) and length of 153ft 4in (46.74m). The latter figure was for a circular-section fuselage carrying most of the fuel, which provided an estimated range of 3,000nm (3,455 miles; 5,559km) at a maximum take-off weight of 45,705lb (20,732kg).

The parallel CL-325-2 design was slightly smaller and lighter, and was planned for comparable performance with the aid of fuel carried in drop tanks. The USAF thought that Garrett could not bring the Rex III engine to fruition, and in October 1957 cancelled Garrett's development contracts.

However, this subcontract work had fired the enthusiasm of Lockheed for hydrogen-fuelled aircraft able to operate at extreme altitudes, and in January 1956 Lockheed offered to build two prototypes, the first of them to fly within 18 months of contract signature. The USAF was highly interested and contacted both General Electric and Pratt & Whitney for hydrogen-fuelled engine proposals. The latter was selected, and Lockheed designed its two-seat CL-400 to an April 1956 contract with a long circular-section fuselage carrying a mid-set wing of trapezoidal planform and a tall T-tail with a ventral fin. The type perched on a tricycle landing gear arrangement with a twin-wheel nose unit and single-wheel main units that folded into fairings below the two tip-mounted nacelles. These each carried one Pratt & Whitney 304-2 hydrogen-fuelled turbojet rated at 9,500lb st

(42.26kN) with afterburning, and an enormous fuel capacity of 29,977 Imp gal (136,274 litres) in three fuselage tanks was calculated to provide a range of 1,900nm (2,188 miles; 3,521km) at a cruising speed of 1,435kt (1,653mph; 2,660km/h) or Mach 2.5 at 100,000ft (30,480m). Other data included a span of 83ft 9in (25.53m), length of 164ft 10in (50.24m) and maximum take-off weight of 69,955lb (31,731kg).

As construction of the first machine proceeded, Lockheed became increasingly concerned at the CL-400's comparatively short range with vast quantities of fuel, and at the instigation of chief designer Clarence 'Kelly' Johnson persuaded the USAF to cancel work in October 1957 even though the first prototype was nearly complete. During this year the USSR orbited the world's first artificial satellite, and although the USAF and Central Intelligence Agency agreed that the satellite would become the reconnaissance platform of the future, they also agreed that there would still be a need for reconnaissance aircraft to provide a rapid-reaction reconnaissance capability. At the behest of the CIA, therefore, the USAF contracted with Lockheed and General Dynamics for reconnaissance aeroplane concepts offering very high performance.

This time, Johnson and his design team decided to use well-proved engine technology, and chose the Pratt & Whitney JT11D bleed turbojet that was under development for military service as the J58. After it had examined the design concepts, the USAF selected the Lockheed 'Oxcart' type in preference to two related General Dynamics' aircraft, the two-seat 'Fish' and 'Kingfish' ogival delta-winged types conceived for Mach 6 performance with ramjet propulsion.

Lockheed was selected to proceed on the basis of its twelfth design proposal, which the CIA selected via the USAF as the production variant with the designation A-12; A stood for Article, which was CIA terminology for any of its own aircraft. As it was designed to reach the speeds at which aerodynamic heating of the airframe would cause the failure of conventional aluminium alloys, the airframe was built almost exclusively of titanium alloys, whose expansion and contraction during flight dictated the incorporation of chordwise corrugations on the inner panels of the wing and expansion gaps between other panels: this was one of the reasons that the A-12 and its successors dripped fuel on the ground, the integral tankage becoming fluid-tight only after it had expanded in high-speed flight. Further reduction in the effect of aerodynamic heating was provided by the very dark blue paint in which the aircraft were finished, this paint radiating heat at some 2.5 times the rate of unpainted titanium alloy.

The design was based on a circular-section fuselage carrying, from nose to tail, optical reconnaissance equipment, the cockpit section and its associated environmental equipment, more reconnaissance equipment in the so-called 'Q-bay', the two-wheel nose unit of the tricycle landing gear, and much of the internal fuel. The short-span delta wing was located at the rear of the fuselage and was supplemented by long chines extending right to the nose, thus providing a measure of yaw-damping in high-speed flight as well as additional volume for fuel and bays for palletised electronic reconnaissance equipment. The wing supported the two three-wheel main landing gear units and the two vast engine nacelles, each surmounted by one of the inward-canted vertical tail surfaces. Each engine installation was a wonder in its own right, and located the engine in a complex inlet and ejector system that allowed it to operate at maximum efficiency. Such was the nature of the powerplant installation that the engine supplied all the power in turbojet form at low speed, this situation changing gradually so that, at Mach 3.2, the engine was operating in turbo-ramjet form (with much of the inlet air ducted around the compressor section for dumping into the afterburner face) and delivering only 17.6 per cent of the power, the remaining 82.4 per cent being supplied by inlet suction (54 per cent) and ejector thrust (28.4 per cent).

Production of this single-seat variant totalled 15 aircraft. In other respects, the A-12 differed from the SR-71A in its length of 98ft 9in (30.10m) increasing to 102ft 0in (31.09m) with the pitot boom; empty weight of about 60,000lb (27,216kg); maximum take-off weight of about 120,000lb (54,432kg); maximum level speed 'clean' of 2,085kt (2,402mph; 3,865km/h) or Mach 3.64 at 92,500ft (28,194m); range of 2,175nm (2,505 miles; 4,031km), and service ceiling of 95,000ft (28,955m).

The first A-12 flew in April 1962 with a temporary powerplant of two Pratt & Whitney J75 turbojets, and development proved difficult because of the complexity of

The Lockheed Martin SR-71 carries a mass of highly
classified optical, thermal and electronic
reconnaissance equipment that is located mostly in
the long chines extending forward from the wing roots
to the nose.

the A-12's systems, in particular the powerplant installation. One other machine was built in two-seat pilot conversion trainer layout with a raised second cockpit in the 'Q-bay' position, and this model was powered by J75 turbojets for a maximum speed of Mach 1.2. Some of the aircraft may have been used operationally, although most were allocated to various development tasks.

Official confirmation of the A-12's existence came only in February 1964 in an announcement by President Lyndon B. Johnson, and the accompanying information (including a photograph of the YF-12A) wrongly described the machine as the A-11. The A-12 was approaching the end of its useful life by 1967 as more-advanced reconnaissance capabilities became available from satellite imagery, and the last A-12 flight was made in June 1968.

M-12: Soon after beginning work on the A-12, the Lockheed team decided to make the new machine capable of operating as a reconnaissance platform in its own right, or alternatively of serving as a launch and control platform for a remotely piloted reconnaissance vehicle that could be used either to extend the basic aeroplane's reconnaissance range or to operate in areas too dangerous or sensitive for the manned parent platform. For this reason, the 'Skunk Works' (nickname of Lockheed's Advanced Development Projects section) now proceeded on the parallel design and development of the manned platform and the D-21 drone. It was decided that the best position to carry the drone was above the fuselage, and this was one of the factors that resulted in the vertical tail surfaces above the engines, rather than a single surface above the rear fuselage.

The drone-carrier variant was the M-12, of which two were produced as A-12 conversions with the 'Q-bay' volume used for the seat and equipment needed by the drone operator. The D-21 drone was based on the same blended wing/chine aerodynamics as the A-12, but had a single fuselage-mounted engine, a camera bay just aft of the inlet in the lower part of the fuselage, and a single vertical tail surface. The D-21 was powered by a Marquardt RJ43-MA-11 ramjet rated at about 11,500lb st (51.15kN), spanned 19ft 0in (5.79m) and was 43ft 2in (13.16m) long, possessed a maximum weight of 20,000lb (9,072kg), and could cruise at Mach 4.

The drone was carried on a simple pylon above the rear fuselage in line with the M-12's vertical tail surfaces, and was designed to fly at the end of its mission to a predetermined position before ejecting its sensor package. This parachute-equipped package was recovered in the air by a Lockheed JC-130B Hercules, while the expendable D-21 was destroyed by explosives either in the air or after contact with the ground or water. It is believed that some 38 D-21 drones were built, but problems with launching the drone from the M-12 (resulting in the loss of one launch aeroplane) meant that the few operational missions flown by the D-21 between 1964 and mid-1967 were launched from two converted Boeing B-52H Stratofortress bombers.

SR-71A: In July 1964, President Johnson announced that Lockheed was developing an advanced strategic reconnaissance platform. This was the next in sequence after the planned RS-70 reconnaissance derivative of the North American B-70 Valkyrie Mach 3 bomber, but the President read his briefing notes wrongly and referred to the new machine as the SR-71, and this official mistake was allowed to stand.

By this time the first SR-71A was approaching completion as the leader of an initial batch of six aircraft ordered by the USAF in December 1962, and to an improved A-12 standard for the strategic reconnaissance role with an internal fuel capacity of 1,158.8 Imp gal (46,181.9 litres), increased weights, and slightly more length to allow the incorporation of additional reconnaissance equipment as well as two more comfortable cockpits based on the two-seat accommodation of the M-12.

This first machine flew in December 1964, and the SR-71A entered service in January 1966. Production totalled 32 aircraft, including one diverted to NASA on permanent loan with the fictitious designation YF-12C.

The SR-71A was retired in the early 1990s, but in the mid-1990s three aircraft were restored to flight status as a result of Congressional pressure.

SR-71B: This was a single conversion from SR-71A standard as a two-seat pilot trainer with a raised second cockpit in place of the systems operator's position, and with the under-nacelle fin of the YF-12A.

SR-71C: This was a single conversion from YF-12A standard as a two-seat pilot trainer.

Lockheed Martin U-2 and TR-1

Manufacturer: Lockheed Martin 'Skunk Works' Division of the Lockheed Martin Corporation (originally Lockheed-California Company and later Lockheed Advanced Development Company of the Lockheed Aircraft Corporation)

Country of origin: USA

Specification: TR-1A (U-2R)

Type: Reconnaissance and electronic warfare aeroplane

Accommodation: Pilot on a zero/zero ejector seat

Entered service: 1956

Left service: Still in service

Operational equipment: Standard communication and navigation equipment, plus up to 3,000lb (1,361kg) of classified optical, optronic, IR, and electronic (including Hughes ASARS-2 SLAR or Lockheed Precision Location Strike System radar localiser) reconnaissance systems in one large pressurised 'Q' bay and one small 'E' fuselage bay and two 90cu ft (2.55cu m) wing-mounted unpressurised pods each 27ft 0in (8.23m) long and carrying up to 600lb (272kg) of equipment, ECM system including RWR, drift sight, INS and TACAN

Powerplant: One Pratt & Whitney J75-P-13B turbojet rated at 17,000lb st (75.62kN) dry

Fuel capacity: Internal fuel 7,649lb (3,470kg); external fuel none; no provision for inflight refuelling

Dimensions: Span 103ft 0in (31.39m); aspect ratio about 10.61; area about 1,000.00sq ft (92.90sq m); length 62ft 9in (19.13m); height 16ft 0in (4.88m)

Weights: Empty less than 10,000lb (4,536kg) without powerplant and equipment pods, and about 15,500lb (7,031kg) operating; maximum take-off 41,300lb (18,734kg)

Performance: Cruising speed, maximum more than 373kt (430mph; 692km/h) at 70,000ft (21,335m); range considerably more than 2,605nm (3,000 miles; 4,828km); endurance 12hr 0min; maximum rate of climb at sea level about 5,000ft (1,525m) per minute; climb to 65,000ft (19,810m) in 15 min 0 sec; service ceiling 90,000ft (27,430m)

Variants

U-2A: In the first half of the 1950s the USA's assumption of technological superiority over the USSR was jolted by the detonation of the first Soviet thermonuclear weapon in August 1953, and then by the appearance in May 1954 of a delivery system for this weapon in the form of the Myasishchyev M-4 'Bison' heavy bomber. Consequently, it was clear that American strategic reconnaissance needed new capability to counter the Soviets' technological advances. The key to the required capability came in the development of new high-resolution cameras, advanced lenses and Mylar-based film, by Dr Edwin Land, the Hycon Corporation and Eastman respectively. In concert, these offered the possibility of a very advanced aerial reconnaissance capability, and thoughts now turned to the type of platform that would be needed in order to take maximum advantage of this capability. Current reconnaissance aircraft of the electronic and optical types lacked the altitude performance to operate above the ceiling of Soviet interceptors, so it was clear that long overflights would require a platform able to operate at extremely high altitude.

In March 1953, and fronting for the CIA, the USAF's Wright Air Development Centre finalised the specification for a reconnaissance type with a range of 1,525nm (1,756 miles; 2,826km) and a ceiling of 70,000ft (21,335m) or more with a sensor payload of between 100 and 700lb (45 and 318kg). The USAF issued this 'Bald Eagle' specification to Bell, Fairchild and Martin, subsequently ordering 20 examples of the Martin RB-57D development of the B-57B bomber with a much enlarged wing, and one prototype and 22 production examples of the Bell X-16 which, like the RB-57D, was to be powered by a pair of Pratt & Whitney J57-P-37 turbojets. Although not invited to tender to the specification, Lockheed knew of its existence and as a private venture planned a development of its F-104 Starfighter high-altitude interceptor as the CL-282. This was designed to take-off from a jettisonable dolly (the subsequent landing being effected on extendible skids) and, with a powerplant of one General Electric J73-GE-X52 turbojet rated at 9,300lb st (41.37kN) dry, was expected to be capable of attaining a high altitude as a result of its long wing, which spanned 70ft 8in (21.54m) with an aspect ratio of 9.99 and an area of 500.00sq ft (46.45sq m). The USAF rejected the design, but a presidential committee then decided that the RB-57D lacked the required range and that the X-16 was too great a technical risk. In November 1954, therefore, the CIA secured presidential approval to replace the X-16 with the proposal from Lockheed, which promised a prototype within eight months.

Lockheed entrusted development of the CL-282 to a team headed by Clarence 'Kelly' Johnson of the company's Advanced Developments Projects department, located at the 'Skunk Works' secret design and construction facility in Burbank, California. The team's main task was to provide longer range and greater operating altitude. To this end, the fuselage was redesigned as a lengthened unit with greater internal fuel capacity and the more powerful Pratt & Whitney J57-P-37 turbojet rated at 10,500lb st (46.71kN) dry, and the wing was extended to 80ft 0in (24.38m) for the higher aspect ratio of 11.33 and greater area of 565.00sq ft (52.49sq m). Weight-saving features included a very light structure with a wing that weighed a mere 3lb/sq ft (14.6kg/sq m) – about one-third of the figure for conventional jet aircraft, an S-1010B full-pressure pilot's suit to avoid the need for cabin pressurisation, a conventional seat rather than an ejector seat although such a seat was later fitted, and, in place of the CL-282's skid landing gear, a retractable but lightweight bicycle combination. This last feature comprised twin-wheel main and tail units in tandem under the fuselage, underwing outrigger units that provided stability during the take-off run but were dropped after lift-off, and down-turned wingtips to serve as the skids onto which the wing could subside as it lost lateral control during the last stages of the landing run.

The type was designated in the U-for-utility series to disguise its real role, and the prototype first flew in August 1955. It soon became clear that the U-2 offered exceptional capabilities, and the initial CIA order was soon complemented by a USAF contract. Although early aircraft retained the prototype's J57-P-37 engine, later aircraft were powered by the J57-P-37A turbojet rated at 11,200lb st (49.82kN) dry. The internal fuel capacity was 653.7 Imp gal (2,971.5 litres) supplemented by 174.9 Imp gal (794.9 litres) in two non-jettisonable slipper tanks on the wing leading edges, and up to 750lb (340kg) of reconnaissance equipment could be installed in the 'Q-bay' immediately behind the cockpit.

As the type's service career progressed, the surviving aircraft sprouted a number of additional antennae and radome associated with extra reconnaissance systems. A number of the USAF's U-2A aircraft were later revised to WU-2A standard for the atmospheric research and radiation sampling roles, the latter characterised by a large port-side air scoop beneath the equipment bay.

U-2B: This model was introduced in 1959, probably for use only by the CIA (although possibly by Taiwan at a later date), as a develop-ment of the U-2A with integral wing tankage and a new power-plant in the form of the Pratt & Whitney J75 turbojet. The new tankage raised internal fuel cap-acity to 949.25 Imp gal (4,315.4 litres), and while

early aircraft had the J75-P-13 turbojet rated at 15,800lb st (70.28kN) dry, later aircraft were powered by the J75-P-13B rated at 17,000lb st (75.62 kN) dry. The type was also more difficult to fly than the U-2A, for at high altitude, the additional weight of the engine and fuel meant that the stalling speed was only 4kt (4.6mph; 7.4km/h) below the airframe's limiting Mach number, requiring the pilot to operate within an extraordinarily narrow speed band if his machine was not to enter either of two buffet zones.

Production of the U-2A and U-2B is thought to have totalled at least 48 machines in the form of 20 aircraft for the CIA and 28 aircraft for the USAF. The U-2A made its first overflight of the USSR in July 1956, and the two initial models made many such flights up to May 1960, when a U-2B flown by Francis Gary Powers was brought down near Smolensk by a Soviet SA-2 'Guideline' SAM. This signalled the end of the U-2's invulnerability to the USSR's steadily developing air-defence capability, and placed greater

The Lockheed Martin is difficult to fly, and specialised conversion trainers with a separate instructor cockpit have been produced as the U-2C(T) and the TR-1B that was later redesignated as the U-2R(T).

emphasis on the Lockheed A-12 (see separate Lockheed SR-71 entry), which had been ordered in 1959 as a Mach 3 replacement for the subsonic U-2 with the ability to operate at a higher altitude.

U-2C: An unknown number of this model were produced in the early 1960s as U-2B conversions for the Comint and Elint roles. The powerplant of one J75-P-13B engine was standard, with greater airflow provided by enlarged inlets, and the fuel arrangement was revised to provide an internal capacity of 1,099.1 Imp gal (4,996.7 litres) within a total capacity of 1,274 Imp gal (5,791.7 litres) with the slipper

tanks. The nose was lengthened slightly for additional mission equipment, and further volume was provided by the installation of a long dorsal 'canoe' fairing. The total mission equipment weight was 1,450lb (658kg) comprising 750lb (340kg) in the 'Q-bay', 100lb (45kg) in the 'canoe' fairing, and 600lb (272kg) in the two wing pods. Typical data for the U-2C included a span of 80ft 0in (24.38m) with an aspect ratio of 11.33 and an area of 565.00sq ft (52.49sq m); length of 50ft 0in (15.24m); height of 15ft 0in (4.57m); maximum take-off weight of 22,542lb (10,225kg); cruising speed of 400kt (461mph; 742km/h) at 65,000ft (19,811m); range of 2,500nm (2,879 miles; 4,633km); endurance of 6hr 0min, and operating altitude of 70,000ft (21,335m).

Later in the type's career, one U-2C was converted into a dual-control trainer model as the U-2C(T) with the instructor's cockpit inserted behind and above the standard cockpit, and the outrigger 'pogo' wheels retained in flight.

U-2D: Introduced in 1961 as conversions of at least five U-2As, this was a two-seat version for the high-altitude research role with the 'Q-bay' modified for a capsule carrying the second crew member and additional systems associated with radiation and IR research. One of the aircraft was later converted to U-2C(T) standard.

U-2E: This designation was applied to an unknown number

of U-2A and U-2B conversions for CIA use with improved ECM capability.

U-2F: This designation was applied to an unknown number of U-2A conversions with an inflight-refuelling receptacle in the port wing. Two of the aircraft were further modified with 'ram's horn' antennae for use in the Sigint role during the Vietnam War (American involvement between 1961 and 1973).

U-2G: Under this designation, two U-2Cs were fitted with arrester hooks for carrier compatibility trials.

U-2J: This designation may have been applied to a small number of carrier-compatible conversions employed operationally by the CIA.

U-2R: This was the final production model of the U-2, and was developed in the mid-1960s to overcome the basic U-2 series' mismatch of engine and airframe. The U-2R thus resembles its predecessors in external configuration though with larger overall dimensions, but internally it is a virtually new and completely restressed design carefully matched to the J75 engine. First flown in August 1967 and produced in 1969 and 1970, the 12 aircraft of the U-2R production batch have greater structural strength, an increased-span wing, increased fuel capacity, an improved cockpit with a zero/zero ejector seat for a pilot wearing the S-1031 full-pressure suit, and considerably improved handling characteristics.

The type carries five 70mm cameras for high-resolution photographic reconnaissance, and large pods can be mounted on the wings for additional reconnaissance equipment (a feature carried over to the TR-1 series). There are also at least two U-2Rs configured for the Comint role with a large dorsal radome containing the equipment for real-time transmission of data via a satellite to the relevant analysis facility. These original U-2R aircraft differ from the later U-2R (originally TR-1A) aircraft in a length of 62ft 11in (19.17m), empty weight of 15,100lb (6,849kg), maximum take-off weight of 41,000lb (18,597kg), maximum range of about 5,428nm (6,250 miles; 10,058km), and service ceiling of 80,000ft (24,383m).

Two of the U-2Rs were loaned to the US Navy for temporary conversion to the U-2EP-X configuration for evaluation of the EP-X (electronic patrol - experimental) role, with a slightly shorter nose and slipper payload pods that did not project to the rear of the wing trailing edges. The type had a different avionics suite that included an FLIR sensor. One other U-2R was converted to U-2R(T) two-seat trainer standard.

TR-IA: In the late 1970s the Americans decided to procure extra aircraft of an improved U-2R type, and an additional 37 'Dragon Ladies' were ordered as two NASA-operated ER-2 earth-resources reconnaissance aircraft, two TR-1B two-seat conversion trainers, one U-2R(T) trainer and 32 TR-IA single-seaters. Introduced in the early 1980s as an advanced U-2R, the TR-IA was delivered with more-capable avionics and different secondary systems, and in December 1991 the surviving 23 aircraft were redesignated U-2R, with their sensors located in five areas (the nose for radar, the 'Q-bay' for bulky optical reconnaissance gear, the 'E-bay' for less bulky electronic receiver gear, the underside of the central and rear fuselage for the 'farms' of electronic receiver antennae, and the two wing pods for radars, Elint or other equipment).

Although its original designation indicated a tactical reconnaissance role, the type serves mainly in the strategic role (14 of the surviving aircraft), only nine being configured for the tactical role with the ASARS-2 synthetic-aperture SLAR able to look 30nm (34.2 miles; 55km) into hostile territory. The tactical aircraft can also be fitted (in place of the ASARS-2 radar in an interchangeable nose section) with the Lockheed Precision Location Strike System for the stand-off detection, classification and localisation of hostile radar systems, whose position is then relayed to friendly forces (via data-link equipment carried in the wing pods).

The USAF has decided to re-engine all its U-2Rs with the General Electric F118-GE-100 non-afterburning turbofan, a relation of the F101-GE-102 used in the Northrop B-2 strategic bomber and rated at 19,000lb st (84.51kN) dry. The engine is lighter and more powerful than the current J75 turbojet, and in addition to easing logistic problems will provide better climb rate, higher ceiling, and still greater range.

TR-IB: This is the two-seat conversion trainer variant of the TR-IA. Two aircraft were built to this standard, but in December 1991 the designation was changed to U-2R(T).

McDonnell Douglas RF-4 Phantom II

Manufacturer: McDonnell Aircraft Company of the McDonnell Douglas Corporation (originally McDonnell Aircraft Corporation)

Country of origin: USA

Specification: RF-4C Phantom II

Type: Multi-role reconnaissance aeroplane

Accommodation: Pilot and systems operator in tandem on Martin-Baker Mk H7 zero/zero ejector seats

Entered service: (F-4 series) 1961

Left service: Still in service

Operational equipment: Standard communication and navigation equipment, plus ASQ-19(B) communication, navigation and identification package, CKP-92A/A24G-34 central air-data computer, APQ-99 radar, ASQ-88B weapon-release system (although weapons are seldom carried), ASQ-90 data display, AAS-18 IR receiver, APR-25 homing and warning receiver, ALR-17 ECM receiver, podded countermeasures such as the ALQ-101, ALQ-119, ALQ-130, ALQ-131 and Northrop ALQ-184 radar jammers, the Loral ALQ-123, Sanders ALQ-140 and Northrop AAQ-8 IR jammers, and the Magnavox ALW-108 IFF jammer, ASN-56 INS and ASN-46A navigation computer, APQ-102 side-looking airborne radar, and a comprehensive array of alternative camera installations including high- and low-altitude panoramic cameras as well as forward-facing and oblique cameras in the front, centre and rear positions

Powerplant: Two General Electric J79-GE-15 turbojets each rated at 10,900lb st (48.49kN) dry and 17,000lb st (75.62kN) with afterburning

Fuel capacity: Internal fuel 12,290lb (5,575kg); external fuel up to 8,830lb (4,005kg) in one 499.6 Imp gal (2,271.2

litre) and two 308.1 Imp gal (1,400.6 litre) drop tanks; provision for inflight refuelling

Dimensions: Span 38ft 4.875in (11.71m) and width folded 27ft 6in (8.38m); aspect ratio 2.82; area 530.00sq ft (49.24sq m); length 62ft 11in (19.17m); height 16ft 5.5in (5.02m); tailplane span 17ft 11.5in (5.47m); wheel track 17ft 10.5in (5.30m); wheelbase 23ft 4.5in (7.12m)

Weights: Empty 28,276lb (12,826kg); maximum take-off 58,000lb (26,309kg)

Performance: Maximum level speed 'clean' 1,267kt (1,460mph; 2,349km/h) or Mach 2.21 at 40,000ft (12,191m); ferry range 1,520nm (1,750 miles; 2,816km) with drop tanks; radius 729nm (840 miles; 1,352km); maximum rate of climb at sea level 48,000ft (14,630m) per minute; service ceiling 59,400ft (18,105m)

Variants

RF-4B Phantom II: By any criterion, one of the most important warplanes ever produced and the only Western warplane to be built in numbers exceeding 5,000 since World War II, the Phantom II is still in comparatively widespread service during the mid-1990s but is approaching obsolescence and is scheduled for retirement by the beginning of the next century. The origins of the Phantom II can be traced back to June 1953, when the US Navy contracted with Vought rather than McDonnell for its next carrierborne fighter. The St Louis-based company was

The McDonnell Douglas F-4 Phantom II has been one of the great warplanes of all time, and is seen here in the form of an F-4E of the Israeli air force, which also operates the type in its RF-4E dedicated reconnaissance form for optical, thermal and electronic intelligence-gathering.

disappointed, for it had supplied three previous generations of turbojet-powered fighters to the US Navy and had put all its experience with these three types (together with the F-101 Voodoo for the USAF) into the preliminary design for the type intended as the US Navy's first supersonic fighter.

The carrierborne fighter was still the company's prime interest, however, so McDonnell started work on the concept for a more advanced type and set about the difficult process of convincing the US Navy of the new concept's value as an all-weather fighter. In 1954, McDonnell created a mock-up of this F3H-G/H single-seat fighter with an inbuilt armament of four 20mm cannon, provision for a comparatively large but long-ranged nose radar, 11 external hardpoints, and a powerplant of two Wright J65 turbojets. This engine type was an American development of a British turbojet, the Armstrong Siddeley Sapphire, and the use of two such engines in the large F3H-G/H promised a maximum speed in the order of Mach 1.5 at altitude. The F3H-G/H mock-up was very impressive, and in October 1954 the US Navy issued a letter of intent to buy two YAH-1 prototypes of an F3H-G/H version optimised for the carrierborne attack role with a powerplant of two more-powerful General Electric J79 turbojets. In April 1955, however, the company lost six months of design effort when the US Navy changed its mind and ordered the completion of the two prototypes as XF4H-I all-weather fighter prototypes.

This necessitated a considerable redesign, for the new requirement demanded the ability to detect, intercept and destroy incoming enemy warplanes during the course of a two-hour combat air patrol at a radius of 250nm (288 miles; 463km). The mission endurance of three hours meant that considerably greater fuel capacity had to be incorporated into the basic design, together with a longer cockpit that had to accommodate the radar intercept officer for the powerful radar fire-control system now required as part of the US Navy's desire for missile rather than cannon armament.

McDonnell revised its basic design, with semi-recessed positions under the fuselage for four AAM-N-6 (from September 1962 AIM-7) Sparrow III medium-range AAMs with semi-active radar guidance, and only one hardpoint. This was located under the fuselage for the carriage of a large drop tank. The first definitive contract, placed in July 1955, covered the two XF4H-I prototypes and five F4H-IF pre-production aircraft for use in the development and service trials role. During November of the same year, mock-up inspection revealed that McDonnell's concept at that time envisaged the use of a thin wing of constant anhedral and a quarter-chord sweep angle of 45 degrees, a powerplant of two J79 afterburning turbojets aspirated via two fixed cheek inlets, and sophisticated avionics managed by the specialist operator located in tandem behind the pilot (each member of the crew being seated on a Martin-Baker Mk H5 ejector seat).

Named Phantom II in July 1959, the F4H was thus the USA's first all-missile fighter with a radar fire-control system that removed, for the first time in a naval fighter, the need for surface radar assistance. Performance was thus optimised for climb rate, speed and range, and estimates of flight characteristics suggested Mach 2+ performance. Wind tunnel tests then revealed that the F4H would be unstable in its currently envisaged form, so the design was recast with a wing based on flat inner panels supporting dogtoothed outer panels set at a dihedral angle of 12 degrees and designed to fold upwards for reduced carrierborne width, slab tailplane halves set at an anhedral angle of 23 degrees to provide additional surface area for directional stability especially at high angles of attack, and engine aspiration via variable-geometry inlets.

*The reconnaissance variants of the McDonnell Douglas F-4
Phantom II series usually have a slightly lengthened nose, with a
smaller radar and with no internal cannon, to provide the
volume required for the dedicated reconnaissance equipment.*

Prototype construction was authorised in December
1956, and the first XF4H-1 was completed in April 1958. A
powerplant of two J79-GE-8 turbojets had been planned,
but development of this engine model had been delayed and
the prototype was therefore fitted with two J79-GE-3A
turbojets loaned by the USAF, and each rated at 9,300lb st
(41.37kN) dry and 14,800lb st (65.83kN) with afterburning.
The XF4H-1 first flew in May 1958, and flight trials revealed
the need for little change except in the angle of the air
inlets. The XF4H-1 was competitively evaluated against the
single-engined Vought XF8U-3 Crusader III and was found
to be superior. The US Navy had already placed an order for
16 more F4H-1s and now contracted for a further 24
warplanes of the same model as pilot production machines,
and in December 1958 ordered the start of full production
with a contract for 375 more aircraft. The planned J79-GE-
8 turbojet was still not available, so the first 45 aircraft (five
service trials and 40 pilot production machines) were
completed with a powerplant of two J79-GE-2 or -2A
turbojets each rated at 10,350lb st (46.04kN) dry and
16,150lb st (71.83kN) with afterburning, and in this form the
variant was designated F4H-1F Phantom II (this designation
being changed to F-4A Phantom II in the September 1962
rationalisation of the US tri-service designation systems).

The F-4B Phantom II was the first true production

The McDonnell Douglas F-4 Phantom II series is now obsolescent in its primary roles, but still offers a considerable capability in the reconnaissance task. Areas and objects for optical and/or thermal imaging are acquired by the pilot with his normal sight.

model of the Phantom II, and started life as the F4H-1 Phantom II development of the late-version F4H-1F with a powerplant of two J79-GE-8 turbojets, each rated at 10,900lb st (48.49kN) dry and 17,000lb st (75.62kN) dry, and supplied with fuel from an internal capacity of 1,642.1 Imp gal (7,464.8 litres) provided by two integral wing tanks and six fuselage bladder tanks.

The type was built for the US Navy and US Marine Corps as a carrierborne fighter and tactical attack warplane, and after a first flight in March 1961, some 649 aircraft were delivered between June 1961 and March 1967.

Ordered in February 1963 on the basis of an earlier F4H-1P proposal, and retired in the early 1990s as the last Phantom II model in first-line service with the US Marine Corps, the RF-4B initially flew in March 1965 as the tactical day/night photo-reconnaissance counterpart of the F-4B fighter. This model had no armament capability, and the F-4B's radar and specialised avionics were replaced by a suite of reconnaissance equipment in a nose section lengthened by 4ft 8.25in (1.43m) for an overall length of 63ft 0in (19.20m). The specialised reconnaissance equipment comprised forward- and side-oblique cameras (or alternatively a mapping camera), supplemented by upward-fired photoflash cartridges for night photography, SLAR and IR sensors. The camera film could be developed in flight and the film cassettes ejected at low altitude for rapid recovery of data by ground teams.

Delivery of 46 aircraft continued from May 1965 to December 1970, and from 1978 the SURE program updated 30 of the aircraft with ASN-92 CAINS (carrier aircraft INS), APD-10 SLAR, Honeywell AAD-5 IR reconnaissance and ALQ-26 ECM systems.

RF-4C Phantom II: In 1961 the USAF evaluated the F4H-1F as a possible successor to the Convair F-106A Delta Dart as the primary interceptor of its Air Defense Command. Although initially reluctant to consider a warplane of naval origins, the service had been impressed by the Phantom II's spate of world records, and was also acting under pressure from Secretary of Defense Robert McNamara, who saw a great opportunity to reduce defence costs by increased inter-service commonality of equipment. Trials revealed that the F4H-1F carried a heavier warload over a greater range than the F-106A, and had a radar offering 25 per cent longer detection range whilst requiring only 70 per cent of the maintenance man-hours needed by the F-106A's radar. Such were the capabilities of the Phantom II, therefore, that in March 1962 the Department of Defense announced that the F110 version of the Phantom II was to become the standard tactical fighter and reconnaissance warplane of the USAF's Tactical Air Command, US Air Forces in Europe and Pacific Air Force. In March 1962, McDonnell accordingly received an initial contract for one F-110A tactical fighter and two YRF-110A reconnaissance aircraft for service trials. In September 1962, the two types were redesignated as the F-4C and RF-4C respectively, and production was authorised in December 1962.

The F-4C was the limited-change equivalent of the F-4B, retaining the naval fighter's wing-folding mechanism and arrester hook. Changes included an inflight-refuelling receptacle on the upper side of the central fuselage, wider wheels with low-pressure tyres, a revised avionics suite (including the APQ-100 radar, AJB-7 all-altitude bombing system, ASN-48 INS, ASN-46 navigation computer, and several system changes including revision to the armament control system for ASM capability), and a powerplant of two J79-GE-15 turbojets each rated at 10,900lb st (48.49kN) dry and 17,000lb st (75.62kN) with afterburning, and equipped with cartridge starters for self-start capability. The first F-4C flew in May 1963, and 583 aircraft were delivered to the USAF between November 1963 and February 1967.

Making its maiden flight in August 1963, the first of two YRF-4C Phantom II aircraft paved the way for the RF-4C tactical reconnaissance version of the F-4C, of which 503 were delivered between April 1964 and January 1974. This variant had the F-4C's missile and bomb delivery systems removed and the nose modified and lengthened by 2ft 9in (0.84m) to produce an overall length of 62ft 11in (19.17m). Optimised for the all-weather day and night reconnaissance role at high and low altitudes, the RF-4C in its initial form was generally equivalent to the RF-4B but had a mission suite that included Texas Instruments APQ-99 (later upgraded to APQ-172) forward-looking radar, AAS-18A IR linescanner, high- and low-altitude panoramic, forward and oblique cameras, and a data-link for real-time downloading of tactically important reconnaissance data.

Some 16 of the aircraft were later upgraded with the APQ-102 SLAR, a further 24 with the Litton ALQ-125 TEREC (tactical electronic reconnaissance) package for detection, identification and localisation of air-defence radars, and another 24 with the LOROP (long-range oblique photography) suite including the KS-127 camera. The RF-4C also has the ARN-101 digital avionics navigation/-reconnaissance system (later upgraded with a more advanced navigation/weapons release system and a ring-laser gyro), ALR-17 ECM receiver, APR-25 homing and warning system, Northrop AAQ-4(V) IR jammer, Northrop ALQ-162 radar jammer, and provision for podded items such as the ALQ-71, -72 and -87 ECM systems that were later replaced by the more modern Westinghouse ALQ-101 and subsequent ECM systems.

A few aircraft surplus to USAF requirements were later transferred to US allies, and of these the South Korean aircraft have been upgraded with a more modern RWR, a Tracor ALE-40 chaff/flare dispenser, and a Westinghouse ALQ-131(V) radar jammer pod.

RF-4E Phantom II: Requiring an improved F-4C more fully optimised for its needs, the USAF contracted in March 1964 for the F-4D variant, of which 793 were delivered between March 1966 and February 1968. This model first flew in December 1965 with avionics tailored to USAF needs and including APQ-109A radar, ASG-22 lead-computing gyro sight, ASQ-91 weapon-release computer

Of the two main British variants of the McDonnell Douglas F-4 Phantom II, the Phantom FGR.Mk 2 can be fitted with a flush-fitting EMI reconnaissance pod under the fuselage.

and ASN-63 INS. However, the USAF was unhappy with the fact that the Phantom II carried no inbuilt cannon, for such a weapon provided useful close-in capability if the opposing warplane managed to close to a point inside the AIM-9 Sidewinder's minimum engagement range and draw the Phantom II into turning combat. An interim solution had been found in the installation of a General Electric SUU-16/A or -23/A pod (each containing one 20mm General Electric M61A1 Vulcan rotary six-barrel cannon and ammunition) on the centreline hardpoint under the fuselage, but the lack of a fully rigid mounting reduced weapon-aiming accuracy to an unfortunate degree.

Design work on a cannon-armed F-4D began in June 1965, and initial assessment revealed that the nose section was not large enough to accommodate the M61A1 cannon. It was thus decided to use the larger nose section of the RF-4C with the cannon faired into a semi-external pod in its lower section. An initial batch of 99 such F-4E fighters was ordered in August 1966, and the first production machine flew during June 1967 as a prelude to a production programme that saw the delivery of 831 F-4E multi-role fighters between October 1967 and December 1976, as well as large numbers of aircraft to allied air forces.

The RF-4E Phantom II is the tactical reconnaissance counterpart of the F-4E, and was designed for the export market with basically the same mission systems as the RF-4C. The first RF-4E flew in September 1970, and production totalled 144 aircraft for Greece, Iran, Israel, Japan (RF-4EJ Phantom II), Turkey and West Germany.

Northrop Grumman (General Dynamics) EF-111 Raven

Manufacturer: General Dynamics Corporation and Northrop Grumman Corporation (originally Grumman Aircraft Engineering Corporation, and later Grumman Aircraft Group of the Grumman Corporation)

Country of origin: USA

Specification: EF-111 Raven

Type: Variable-geometry all-weather electronic warfare aeroplane

Accommodation: Pilot and systems operator side-by-side in a McDonnell Douglas zero/zero escape module

Entered service: (F-111 series) June 1967

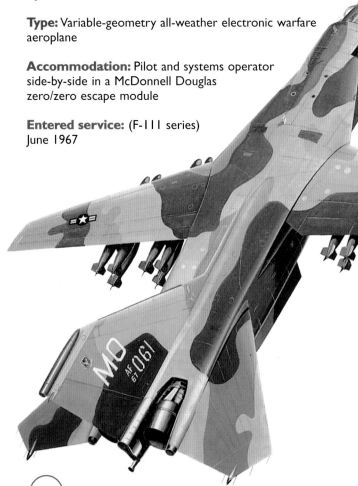

Left service: Still in service

Operational equipment: Standard communication and navigation equipment, plus General Electric APQ-160 navigation radar, APQ-110 terrain-following radar, Litton AJN-16 INS, Raytheon ALQ-99E(V) TJS, ALQ-137(V)4 deception jammer, Dalmo-Victor ALR-62(V)4 terminal threat-warning receiver, Tracor ALE-40 chaff/flare dispenser, ALR-23 countermeasures receiver system, and ALQ-131 jammer system in pods under the wings, and GPL Doppler navigation

Powerplant: Two Pratt & Whitney TF30-P-3 turbofans each rated at 11,500lb st (51.15kN) dry and 18,500lb st (82.29kN) with afterburning

Fuel capacity: Internal fuel 32,493lb (14,739kg); external fuel up to four 499.6 Imp gal (2,271.25 litre) drop tanks; provision for inflight refuelling

Dimensions: Span 63ft 0in (19.20m) spread and 31ft 11.4in (9.74m) swept; aspect ratio 7.56 spread and 1.55 swept; area 525.00sq ft (48.77sq m) spread and 657.07sq ft (61.07sq m) swept; length 76ft 0in (23.16m); height 20ft 0in (6.10m)

Weights: Empty 55,275lb (25,073kg) operating; normal take-off 70,000lb (31,752kg); maximum take-off 88,948lb (40,347kg)

Performance: Maximum level speed 'clean' 1,226kt (1,412mph; 2,272km/h) or Mach 2.14 at high altitude; maximum combat speed 1,196kt (1,377mph; 2,216km/h) or Mach 2.085 at high altitude; average speed in the combat area 507kt (584mph; 940km/h) at optimum

The General Dynamics F-111 was schemed as a long-range strike fighter for the USAF and as a fleet-defence fighter for the US Navy, but entered service only in the former role for service up to 1996, when the only variant left in American service was the EF-111A Raven electronic warfare model.

altitude; radius 807nm (929 miles; 1,495km); unrefuelled endurance more than 4hr 0min; maximum rate of climb at sea level 3,300ft (1,006m) per minute; service ceiling 45,000ft (13,715m)

Variants

EF-111A Raven: The F-111 was the world's first variable-geometry warplane to enter production and service. The type's origins can be traced back to the later 1950s, when the USAF started to consider the type of warplane that could succeed the Republic F-105 Thunderchief in the nuclear strike role at the tactical and operational levels. The USAF wanted a warplane that could operate at very high speed and exceptionally low level under all weather conditions by day or night, use short lengths of bomb-damaged runway or the smaller runways of dispersal airfields, and fly over long ranges operationally and for deployment to distant overseas bases without the need for large numbers of inflight-refuelling tankers. The USAF initially considered the use of zero-length launching techniques, but the use of a powerful booster rocket for take-off from an inclined ramp was expensive and did not obviate the need for a long runway on which to land; VTOL was still unproved and would demand powerful engines whose fuel consumption would erode both ferry range and operational radius.

The service therefore opted for a variable-geometry wing planform as this offered a good blend of capabilities: in the minimum-sweep position such a planform offered good field performance and excellent ferry range, in the intermediate-sweep position it offered a combination of modest speed and modest range, and in the maximum-sweep position it offered very high dash speed and the low gust response required for sustained transonic or supersonic flight at very low level without unacceptable degradation of crew performance. The development of such a wing generated considerable structural and aerodynamic problems, but a successful solution to these problems promised very useful advantages. The benefits of the variable-geometry planform also attracted the interest of politicians, who saw the makings of a type that could satisfy not only the USAF's need but also the US Navy's requirement for a fleet air-defence fighter (to succeed the new McDonnell F4H Phantom II) with STOL capability, high speed, long range and endurance, and considerable weapon load.

In February 1961, therefore, Secretary of Defense Robert McNamara ordered the USAF and US Navy to combine their requirements so that a single airframe/powerplant combination could be used for both the warplanes. The services were far less confident of a successful conclusion for any joint type, but had little choice in the matter and finally agreed on the TFX (Tactical Fighter Experimental) requirement. The variant for the air force was to be capable of undertaking the nuclear strike, conventional interdiction and conventional close air-support roles, and its performance was to include dash speeds of Mach 2.5 and 1.2 at high and low altitudes respectively, an unrefuelled ferry range of 3,300nm (3,800 miles; 6,115km), a radius of 800nm (921 miles; 1,482km) including a supersonic penetration of 200nm (230 miles; 370km) at low level, and the ability to take-off and land over a 50ft (15m) obstacle in less than 3,000ft (914m). The variant for the US Navy, which was forced to drop its planned Douglas F6D Missileer subsonic type, demanded a loiter of 3hr 30min at a radius of 150nm (173 miles; 278km) carrying six 1,000lb (454kg) missiles.

The difficult yet potentially lucrative requirement was issued to US aircraft manufacturers, and by early 1962 the field had been reduced from six contenders to two, in the form of designs from Boeing and General Dynamics. The two designs were not dissimilar, although the Boeing concept made extensive use of titanium in its structure and its powerplant arrangement included thrust reversers as well as inlets on top of the fuselage. The designs each had their particular areas of merit, but the General Dynamics concept offered greater commonality between the USAF and US Navy models, and was therefore selected in preference to the Boeing design. A development contract was issued in November 1962 for the TFX, which now became the F-111. General Dynamics had already teamed with a manufacturer far more experienced in naval warplanes, and Grumman was now made responsible for the F-111B naval version with longer wings increasing minimum-sweep span to 70ft 0in (21.34m) with an aspect ratio of 8.91 and an area of 550.00sq ft (51.10sq m), a shorter nose carrying the completely revised Hughes AWG-9 radar (derived from that of the YF-12A Mach 3 interceptor counterpart of the Lockheed SR-71 reconnaissance platform) and reducing length to 66ft 8.5in (20.33m), and a primary armament of six Hughes AIM-54 Phoenix long-range AAMs.

Given the technical novelties embodied in the type, there were no XF-111 prototypes nor even YF-111 service test aircraft, although development flying was to be undertaken with a fairly large number of initial production aircraft, namely 18 (later reduced to 17) F-111A land-based aircraft and five F-111B carrierborne aircraft. The first F-111A and first F-111B flew in December 1964 and May 1965 respectively, both with a powerplant of two Pratt & Whitney TF30-P-1 turbofans each rated at 11,500lb st (51.15kN) dry and 18,500lb st (82.29kN) with afterburning. The F-111B program was troubled from the start by high drag and excessive weight, and was terminated during May 1968 in favour of the Grumman VFX (Carrierborne Fighter Experimental) proposal that matured as the F-14 Tomcat fleet-defence fighter.

Greater success attended the F-111A land-based model, which suffered a number of teething problems but then matured as a truly exceptional warplane. After protracted development, the F-111A was delivered to the USAF's TAC from June 1967 even though there were still many problems with the advanced airframe, the temperamental engine type that suffered from a compressor stall tendency, and the complex avionics. Production of the F-111A totalled 141 aircraft with a powerplant of two TF30-P-3 turbofans each rated at 12,000lb st (53.38kN) dry and 18,500lb st (82.29kN) with afterburning.

Considerable trouble had been experienced during development flying with the two quarter-cone multi-shock inlets, which combined with rapid changes in the cross-section of the trunking between each inlet and its associated engine to produce serious distortion in the airflow and consequent engine surging. The problem was cured by changes in the TF30-P-3 engine and adoption of Triple Plow 1 inlets with vortex generators and three diverters for the fuselage boundary-layer air.

EF-111A Raven is the designation applied to 42 electronic warfare aircraft produced by Grumman as F-111A conversions and colloquially known as 'Spark Vark' or 'Electric Fox' machines. Such a version was proposed as early as 1970 as replacement for the Douglas EB-66 Destroyer, but it was only in January 1975 that Grumman was contracted to produce two prototype conversions. The first of these flew in December 1975, with a 'canoe' fairing (16ft 0in/4.88m in length) under the fuselage for the Raytheon TJS of the Grumman EA-6B Prowler

The Northrop Grumman (General Electric) EF-111A Raven bears a close external resemblance to the F-111A except for the large fin-top fairing that carries the forward-, side- and rear-facing antennae for the ALQ-99E Tactical Jamming System that is packaged into the erstwhile lower-fuselage weapons bay, which is now covered by a large 'canoe' fairing to provide additional volume for the TJS's six digitally tuned receivers, five exciters and 10 jamming transmitters.

repackaged in ALQ-99E(V) computer-assisted form for one-man operation, and possessing sufficient power to overwhelm the world's most intense radar defences. The 'canoe' fairing is located over the erstwhile weapons bay, this arrangement accommodating the TJS and its six digitally-tuned receivers, five exciters and 10 jamming transmitters. The system also includes a number of forward-, side- and rearward-facing receiver antennae located in a large, bulged fairing at the top of the vertical tail surface, with the control section located in the starboard side of the cockpit for the electronic warfare officer who constitutes the second member of the crew. Other systems are the ALQ-137(V)4 deception jammer, Dalmo-Victor ALR-62(V)4 terminal threat-warning receiver, Tracor ALE-40 chaff/flare dispenser, ALR-23 countermeasures receiver system, and (for possible retrofit) ALQ-131 jammer system in pods under the wings. With this advanced suite of mission equipment, the Raven can support tactical warplanes as an escort, in the penetration role, or as a stand-off jammer. The ALQ-99E electronic system is being upgraded in concert with the ALQ-99 system of the EA-6B, and the EF-111A may be retrofitted to carry the AGM-88 HARM anti-radar missile on its four underwing hardpoints.

Northrop Grumman E-2 Hawkeye

Manufacturer: Northrop Grumman Corporation (originally Grumman Aircraft Engineering Corporation, and later Grumman Aircraft Group of the Grumman Corporation)

Country of origin: USA

Specification: E-2C Hawkeye

Type: Carrierborne and land-based airborne early warning aeroplane

Accommodation: Pilot and co-pilot side-by-side, and a mission crew of three carried in the cabin

Entered service: January 1964

Left service: Still in service

Operational equipment: Standard communication and navigation equipment, plus GEC-Marconi air-data computer and Litton L-304 central computer system, Lockheed Martin (originally General Electric) APS-125, or (from 1983 production) APS-138 or (from 1988 production and for retrofit in older aircraft) APS-139, or (from 1991 production) APS-145 surveillance radar with its antenna in a Randtron APA-171 rotodome, Litton ALR-59 or, in later aircraft, Litton ALR-73 ESM and provision for podded items such as the Magnavox ALW-108 IFF jammer, Hazeltine APA-172 control indicator group, and Litton ASN-92 CAINS, GPS receiver and APN-153(V) Doppler navigation

Powerplant: Two Allison T56-A-425 turboprops each rated at 4,910ehp (3,661ekW) or, from 1989 production, two Allison T56-A-427 turboprops each rated at 5,100ehp (3,803ekW) for take-off

Fuel capacity: Internal fuel 12,400lb (5,625kg); external fuel none; provision for inflight refuelling

Dimensions: Span 80ft 7in (24.56m) and width folded 29ft 4in (8.94m); aspect ratio 9.28; area 700.00sq ft (65.03sq m); length 57ft 6.75in (17.54m); height 18ft 3.75in (5.58m); tailplane span 26ft 2.5in (7.99m); wheel track 19ft 5.75in (5.93m); wheelbase 23ft 2in (7.06m)

Weights: Empty 40,484lb (18,363kg); maximum take-off 54,426lb (24,687kg)

Performance: Maximum level speed 'clean' 338kt (389mph; 626km/h) at optimum altitude; cruising speed, maximum 325kt (374mph; 602km/h) at optimum altitude and economical 259kt (298mph; 479km/h) at optimum altitude; ferry range 1,541nm (1,773 miles; 2,853km); radius 175nm (200 miles; 322km) for a patrol of 4hr 24min; endurance 6hr 6min with maximum fuel; maximum rate of climb at sea level 2,515ft (767m) per minute; service ceiling 37,000ft (11,277m)

The Northrop Grumman E-2 Hawkeye is a notably compact airborne early warning and control system platform that is fully carrier-compatible and provides the US Navy with a highly capable long-endurance system for the detection of threats to surface battle groups.

Variants

E-2A Hawkeye: Although at the end of 1955 it ordered the Grumman G-117 design as the WF-2 Tracer carrierborne AEW platform, the US Navy was well aware that this piston-engined type could be only an interim measure pending the design and development of a considerably more advanced turbine-engined type.

TE-2A Hawkeye: This designation was applied to four of the aircraft that were later stripped of their electronic equipment, which was replaced by ballast, for use as pilot trainers.

E-2B Hawkeye: The E-2B was introduced in 1969 by converting E-2As, first with the Litton L-304 software-programmable digital computer in place of the original ASA-27 computer and then with the more capable APS-120 radar that added an overland capacity to the APS-96's basic overwater capability. The first conversion was flown in February 1969, and the conversion programme extended to 49 E-2As that re-entered service from November 1970 with the designation E-2B. The type also introduced an inflight-refuelling capability, and has now been withdrawn from service.

E-2C Hawkeye: This is the definitive version of the Hawkeye, and entered service in November 1973. Development of the type was authorised in April 1968 with the object of giving operational squadrons a Hawkeye model that offered improved detection capability, reliability, and maintainability. The original target was 175 such aircraft, but the total was trimmed to 145 machines in early in 1991 and then further curtailed to 139 aircraft in January 1992 before further orders were placed in December 1994 to raise the total in prospect for the US Navy to 146 aircraft.

Two YE-2C prototypes were created as E-2A conversions, and the first of them flew in January 1971 with a powerplant of two T56-A-422 turboprops each rated at 4,860ehp (3,624ekW). This paved the way for the production model, which first flew in September 1972 with a powerplant of two T56-A-425 turboprops each rated at 4,910ehp (3,661ekW). Other major changes were replacement of the APS-96 radar with its enhanced APS-120 derivative that offered overland as well as overwater capability, the use of the ASN-92 CAINS in place of the

The Northrop Grumman E-2C Hawkeye can detect and track more than 250 air and surface targets at a range of more than 230 miles (371km), and can simultaneously control 30 or more interceptions.

original ASN-36 INS, and the installation of the ALR-59 ESM system for the passive detection of emitting targets; this last feature required the nose to be extended by 1ft 1in (0.33m). The APS-120 radar was later replaced by the General Electric/Grumman APS-125 radar with digital processing and ECCM capability for the detection of aircraft at ranges of 200nm (230 miles; 371km) even in ground clutter, and the simultaneous detection and tracking of more than 250 ship and aircraft targets while controlling 30 or more interceptions at the same time. This radar was introduced from the thirty-fifth E-2C and was then retrofitted on earlier aircraft, and was itself succeeded by three more-advanced equipments in the form of the APS-138 from 1983 with low sidelobes and active-element arrays to permit automatic and simultaneous tracking of up to 600 targets out to a range of 260nm (299 miles; 482km), the APS-139 from 1988 with enhanced capability to detect slow-moving and stationary targets such as warships, and the APS-145 from 1991 for effective operation over normal terrain rather than the comparatively featureless terrain that is the best operating milieu for the Hawkeye's older radars.

From 1980 the aircraft have also featured the improved ALR-73 passive detection system for the automatic detection, plotting and identification of electronic emitters in a high-density environment and at ranges up to 435nm (501 miles; 806km), while the provision of JTIDS data-link equipment allows the secure transmission/reception of information between E-2Cs and other aircraft or surface vessels. Other retrofitted improvement features include colour displays and a GPS receiver for enhanced navigational accuracy.

Grumman has sold the E-2C to Egypt, France, Israel, Japan, Singapore and Taiwan, and also hopes to sell the type to South Korea, Thailand and Turkey.

TE-2C Hawkeye: This is the pilot training version of the E-2C, produced as four conversions of earlier aircraft.

E-2T Hawkeye: This designation is applied to four E-2B aircraft converted to interim E-2C standard for Taiwan, with the APS-138 radar. Grumman flew the first conversion early in 1993, and the other three were converted by AIDC in Taiwan for Taiwanese air force use before the arrival of the service's first new-build E-2Cs in the mid-1990s.

Northrop Grumman EA-6 Prowler

Manufacturer: Northrop Grumman Corporation (originally Grumman Aircraft Engineering Corporation, and later Grumman Aircraft Group of the Grumman Corporation)

Country of origin: USA

Specification: EA-6B Prowler

Type: Carrierborne electronic warfare aeroplane

Accommodation: Pilot, navigator/systems operator and two systems operators in tandem side-by-side pairs on Martin-Baker Mk GRUEA7 zero/zero ejector seats

Entered service: 1972

Left service: Still in service

Operational equipment: Standard communication and navigation equipment, plus central computer, Norden APQ-92 search and NAF APQ-112 mapping radars or (in later aircraft) Norden APQ-130 search and tracking radar, AIL ALQ-99 TJS (variants up to the ALQ-99F in aircraft with updated equipment standards) operating in conjunction with up to five external and self-powered jamming pods, Sanders ALQ-126 deception radar jammer, Rockwell-Collins ASQ-91 communications jammer, Sanders ALQ-149 command and control countermeasures system and two Tracor ALE-39 chaff/flare/decoy dispensers, and Teledyne ASN-123 navigation system; there is provision for up to 4,000lb (1,814kg) of disposable stores carried on four hardpoints all under the wings, with each unit rated at 1,000lb (454kg), and the standard load is four AGM-88 HARM anti-radar missiles

Powerplant: Two Pratt & Whitney J52-P-408 turbojets each rated at 11,200lb st (49.82kN) dry

Fuel capacity: Internal fuel 15,422lb (6,995kg); external fuel up to 10,025lb (4,547kg) in five 333.1 Imp gal (1,514.2 litre) drop tanks; provision for inflight refuelling

Dimensions: Span 53ft 0in (16.15m) and width folded 25ft 10in (7.87m); aspect ratio 5.31; area 528.90sq ft (49.13sq m); length 59ft 10in (18.24m); height 16ft 3in (4.95m); tailplane span 20ft 4.5in (6.21m); wheel track 10ft 10.5in (3.32m); wheelbase 17ft 2in (5.23m)

Weights: Empty 31,572lb (14,321kg); normal take-off 54,461lb (24,703kg) from a carrier in stand-off jamming configuration with five jammer pods, or 60,610lb (27,493kg) from land with maximum internal and external fuel; maximum take-off 65,000lb (29,484kg)

Performance: Maximum level speed 'clean' 566kt (652mph; 1,049km/h) at sea level, or with five jammer pods 530kt (610mph; 981km/h) at sea level; cruising speed 418kt (481mph; 774km/h) at optimum altitude; ferry range 2,085nm (2,399 miles; 3,861km) with empty tanks dropped or 1,756nm (2,022 miles; 3,254km) with empty tanks retained; range 955nm (1,099 miles; 1,769km) with maximum external load; maximum rate of climb at sea level 12,900ft (3,932m) per minute 'clean' or 10,030ft (3,057m) per minute with five jammer pods; service ceiling 41,200ft (12,557m) 'clean' or 38,000ft (11,582m) with five jammer pods

Variants
EA-6B Prowler: Even as the EA-6A Intruder electronic warfare derivative of the Grumman A-6A Intruder carrierborne attack warplane was being developed to meet the US Marine Corps' requirement for a tactical jamming platform, Grumman was preparing a more capable type to

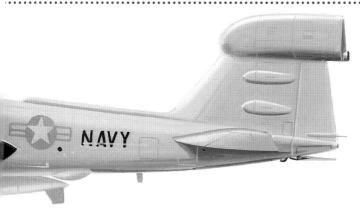

The Northrop Grumman EA-6B Prowler is the US Navy's primary electronic reconnaissance and warfare platform, and was developed from the A-6 Intruder attack warplane with two additional crew members and the advanced Raytheon ALQ-99 Tactical Jamming System with five external jamming pods.

meet an anticipated US Navy requirement. Grumman began work on the improved model in January 1963, and soon concluded that defeat of contemporary Soviet electronic systems would require an automated system that was more advanced than the manually operated system of the EA-6A. In June 1964 the company received official support and funding for more intensive project definition, and by July 1965 had progressed to the stage at which it secured a research and development contract for the TJS (tactical jamming system).

The US Navy issued its requirement in November 1965, and in August 1966 issued Grumman a letter of intent for an A-6 Intruder variant to carry the TJS. Despite its comparatively high level of automation, the TJS still generated too large a quantity of data and demanded too many decisions to be handled by a single electronic countermeasures officer, as in the EA-6A, therefore Grumman decided to lengthen the fuselage of the new type by 4ft 4in (1.32m) so that an additional cockpit section could be added for the side-by-side accommodation of two more electronic countermeasures officers. This meant a reduction in the size of the forward fuselage fuel tank, while the extra wiring required in the wings necessitated a diminution of the wing tankage for a maximum internal capacity of 1,888.5 Imp gal (8,585.3 litres).

Four A-6A airframes were modified as prototypes for

the new EA-6B Prowler, and while the first of these was merely an aerodynamic vehicle, the second was representative of the production standard and flew in May 1968. The first EA-6B off the production line was delivered in January 1971, with a powerplant of two Pratt & Whitney J52-P-8A turbojets each rated at 9,300lb st (41.37kN) dry, but from the twenty-second aeroplane the powerplant became two J52-P-408 turbojets each rated at 11,200lb st (49.82kN) dry. The EA-6B entered service in 1972, and the last of 170 production aircraft was delivered in July 1991. The Prowler remains a key component of the US Navy's attack capability due to a succession of improvement programmes that have enhanced the Prowler's primary electronic system, the ALQ-99 TJS, for the detection, location, classification, and jamming of hostile radars.

The ALQ-99 system uses receiver antennae in the fintop fairing to pick up electromagnetic emissions, and these are then passed to the central digital computer for display and recording before the identity, bearings and jamming set-on frequencies of the emissions are analysed (automatically or manually) and any one of the five external and self-powered jamming pods activated. Each pod covers one of seven frequency bands and contains two powerful jammers.

The first 24 production aircraft were delivered in EA-6B

The Northrop Grumman EA-6B Prowler carries up to five self-powered jammer pods under the fuselage (one) and wings (four), each pod covering one of seven frequency bands and containing two powerful jammers controlled either manually or automatically from the computers of the Tactical Jamming System using data provided by the receivers in the fin-top fairing.

Prowler Standard configuration, with the initial model of the ALQ-99 using the AYA-6 computer to deal only with single emitters in four frequency bands. The next 25 aircraft were delivered from January 1973 in EA-6B Prowler EXCAP (expanded capability) configuration, with the ALQ-99A system (later upgraded to more-reliable ALQ-99B and ALQ-99C standards) for the jamming of radars in eight frequency bands and the capability for automatic coverage of multiple threats; other improvements of this standard were a doubled computer memory, the installation of a digital recorder, and the addition of an Exciter Jammer Control Unit to provide three jammer modes. The following 45 aircraft were delivered from March 1976 in EA-6B Prowler ICAP-1 (improved capability-1) configuration, with the ALQ-99C(V) system using digitally-tuned receivers and computer-controlled subsystems for the jamming of several emitters forming a weapon system; other changes were the replacement of several cockpit displays and controls with a computerised Digital Display Group, provision for new chaff dispenser pods and the ALQ-126A self-protection counter-measure system carried internally in place of the EXCAP standard's ALQ-100 pods, and replacement of the APS-129 search radar by the APS-130 equipment. Some 21 early EA-6B EXCAP aircraft were modified to this standard. Next came 72 aircraft delivered from January 1984 in the EA-6B Prowler ICAP-2 (improved capability-2) configuration first flown in June 1980 with the ALQ-99D(V) system for coverage of a wider frequency range, the AYK-14 computer with four times the memory and three times the speed of the AYA-6, and new and more versatile software for jamming capability in nine frequency bands of several weapon systems forming a defence complex. Other features of the ICAP-2 standard are the installation of the ASN-192 CAINS, deletion of the ASN-152 Doppler navigation, installation of the DECM (defensive electronic countermeasures) suite, and provision for four missiles on four underwing hardpoints. All surviving aircraft of the older configurations have been upgraded to the ICAP-2 configuration.

The final configuration is the EA-6B Prowler ADVCAP (advanced capability), first flown in October 1989 and introduced to service in 1992 at the beginning of a programme to convert 102 ICAP-2 aircraft. The ADVCAP standard introduces the ALQ-99F(V) system using the advanced AYK-14 computer and a more capable Litton/Texas Instruments/ITT receiver/signal processor group operating in 10 frequency bands for improved jamming of communications, four Tracor ALE-47 chaff/-flare/decoy dispensers in place of the baseline model's one (later two) Tracor ALE-39 dispensers, and the Lockheed/ Sanders ALQ-149 TCCS (tactical communications countermeasures system) carried internally but using an underfuselage antenna group for the automatic detection, identification, evaluation and jamming of voice and data communications and long-range early warning radars, and provision for four missiles on the inner four of the six underwing hardpoints; the outer two underwing hardpoints are reserved for ECM pods, and the centreline hardpoint under the fuselage can be used for another ECM pod or a drop tank. Other improvements include a powerplant of two J52-P-409 turbojets each rated at 12,000lb st (53.38kN) dry, APS-130 advanced navigation radar, an improved HUD/HDD display suite, JTIDS, GPS receiver, fin height increased by 1ft 7.75in (0.50m), recontoured flaps and slats, drooped wing leading edges, new forward fuselage strakes, and wingtip air brakes modified to serve as ailerons in conjunction with the digital flight-control system.

Dassault Mirage F1R

Manufacturer: Dassault Aviation (originally Avions Marcel Dassault-Breguet Aviation)

Country of origin: France

Specification: Mirage F1CR-200

Type: All-weather strategic, operational and tactical reconnaissance aeroplane

Accommodation: Pilot on a Hispano-Suiza (Martin-Baker) Mk F1RM4 zero/90kt (104mph; 167km/h) ejector seat or (later aircraft) Hispano-Suiza (Martin-Baker) Mk F10M zero/zero ejector seat

Entered service: (Mirage F1 series) 1973

Left service: Still in service

Operational equipment: Standard communication and navigation equipment, plus Thomson-CSF Cyrano IVMR multi-mode radar, Thomson-CSF VE-120C HUD, Thomson-CSF Sherloc RWR, ECM pods such as the Dassault Electronique Barrax radar jammer, Thomson-CSF Barem, Barracuda, Caïman and Remora radar jammers, and Philips/Matra Phimat and Matra Sycamore chaff/flare launchers, Sagem Uliss 47 INS and Doppler navigation, and a reconnaissance suite including (internal) Omera 33 vertical medium-altitude camera, Omera 40 panoramic camera, Omera 400 sight/recorder, SAT Super Cyclope IR linescanner, Thomson-CSF Raphaël side-looking airborne radar and photoflash installation, and (external) Dassault/Omera Harold reconnaissance pod, Nora pod with optronic sensor, and Thomson-CSF Syrel pod with electronic intelligence sensors; the two wingtip hardpoints can each carry one Matra R550 Magic short-range AAM

Powerplant: One SNECMA Atar 9K-50 turbojet rated at 11,023lb st (49.03kN) dry and 15,785lb st (70.21kN) with afterburning

Fuel capacity: Internal fuel 945.9 Imp gal (4,300 litres);

external fuel up to one 483.9 Imp gal (2,200 litre) or two 248.6 Imp gal (1,130 litre) drop tanks; provision for inflight refuelling

Dimensions: Span 27ft 6.75in (8.40m) without tip stores and about 30ft 6.75in (9.32m) with tip-mounted Magic AAMs; aspect ratio 2.82; area 269.11sq ft (25.00sq m); length 50ft 2.5in (15.30m); height 14ft 9in (4.50m); wheel track 8ft 2.5in (2.50m); wheelbase 16ft 4.75in (5.00m)

Weights: Empty about 17,416lb (7,900kg); maximum take-off 35,715lb (16,200kg)

Performance: Maximum level speed 'clean' 1,262kt (1,454mph; 2,339km/h) or Mach 2.20 at 36,090ft (11,000m); radius 750nm (864 miles; 1,390km) with one reconnaissance pod and two drop tanks; maximum rate of climb at sea level 41,930ft (12,780m) per minute with afterburning; service ceiling 65,615ft (20,000m)

Variants
Mirage F1CR-200: The Mirage III secured considerable commercial success and proved to be a potent warplane in its primary air-defence role, in which its tailless delta configuration and low wing loading were genuine advantages in securing fast climb and high acceleration rates. Few air forces of the period could afford to procure a dedicated interceptor in significant numbers, however, so Dassault was put under great pressure to adapt the initial models to the ground-attack role and to evolve a multi-role attack model as the Mirage IIIE. In these lower-level roles, which involved the carriage of a heavy warload in the type of mission that involved a fair amount of manoeuvring, the tailless delta layout was then found to suffer from the inherent limitations of its high trim drag, download imposed by its elevons in manoeuvring flight, poor field performance, tendency to Dutch roll at high angles of attack, and poor gust response at low level. A partial solution to many of these problems was the adoption of canard foreplanes (as developed separately by IAI and Dassault) to replace the aft download with forward upload and so improve field performance as well as low-level manoeuvrability, but effective multi-role capability demanded a fresh design.

In 1962 Dassault started work on a new warplane that was to be capable of serving both as a Mach 2.2 interceptor at high altitude and as a useful ground-attack warplane, with a low gust response, a combat radius of 302nm (348 miles; 560km), and the ability to operate from comparatively short unpaved runways. The design team considered a number of layouts and powerplants, and several prototypes were flown. Dassault had rejected the conventional swept wing for the Mirage III, as the state of the aeronautical art in the first half of the 1950s dictated a low thickness/chord ratio for the wing of any Mach 2 aircraft, while the state of the structural art made it very difficult to design a conventional swept wing of narrow chord and low thickness/chord ratio.

By the mid-1960s, however, the state of the structural art had developed so considerably that such a wing was now feasible, and Dassault evolved the Mirage IIIF2 (later Mirage F2) design with a conventional fuselage carrying separate wing and tail surfaces. The Mirage F2 was designed for a powerplant of one SNECMA TF-306 turbofan, a French development of the American Pratt & Whitney TF30 engine, and first flew in June 1966. The conventionally winged Mirage F2 was evaluated against Dassault's three other experimental types (the Mirage IIIT tailless delta with the SNECMA TF-106 development of the Pratt & Whitney JTF10A rated at 18,000lb st/80.07kN with afterburning, the Mirage IIIV VTOL tailless delta with a TF-306 thrust engine and eight Rolls-Royce RB.162-2 lift turbojets, and the variable-geometry Mirage IIIG with the TF-306 engine), and emerged as the second best type after the Mirage IIIG.

Although the reasons have never been publicly stated, it seems that the French air force decided not to take the technical risk embodied by the Mirage IIIG (although variable-geometry wing research continued, with a view to using such wings in a replacement for the Mirage IVA strategic nuclear bomber), but to order a smaller version of the Mirage F2 as successor initially to the Sud-Ouest SO.4050 Vautour IIN all-weather interceptor and then to the Mirage III in its interceptor and attack models.

Dassault had already flown the prototype of this Mirage F1 type in December 1966, reasoning that there might be a market for a smaller (and thus cheaper) single-seat type that was based on the well-proved SNECMA Atar turbojet and did not sacrifice too much in the way of performance and operational capability by comparison with the two-seat Mirage F2. The French air force's first step was to order three pre-production Mirage F1 aircraft with the Atar 9K-31 turbojet, and these aircraft made their maiden flights

The Dassault Mirage F1CR-200 is the reconnaissance derivative of the Mirage F1C-200 fighter, with a fixed inflight refuelling probe and a mass of specialised but variable reconnaissance equipment.

between March 1969 and June 1970. The type soon proved that it had better field performance, gust response characteristics and maximum level speed than the Mirage III, together with a 40 per cent improvement in turn rate as a result of its higher aspect ratio wing, and a 200 per cent increase in patrol time as a result of its lower drag and 40 per cent greater internal fuel capacity (careful design resulting in integral rather than bag tanks). The type was also fitted with advanced radar offering 40 per cent greater acquisition range and the possibility of moving target indication. The choice of an elderly French turbojet in place of a modern French development of an advanced American turbofan was initially surprising, but meant that the USA could not veto sales of the warplane for its own political interests at the expense of French commercial interests.

The French air force ordered an initial 30 aircraft in September 1969, and the first of these machines flew as a Mirage F1C fighter in February 1973. Procurement eventually totalled 83 aircraft. The designation Mirage F1C-200 was applied to 79 Mirage F1C fighters of the French air force, with capability for rapid overseas deployment provided by a fixed inflight-refuelling probe whose installation required a lengthening of the fuselage by 3.15in (0.08m) to 50ft 2.5in (15.30m).

The Mirage F1C-200 paved the way for the Mirage

FICR-200, which is the French air force's combat-capable reconnaissance version (64 aircraft) of the Mirage F1C, and was first flown in November 1981 for service from July 1983. The Mirage F1CR-200 retains the fighter's radar and armament capability, although the latter is rarely used, but the radar is the Cyrano IVMR equipment (featuring extra ground mapping, contour mapping, air-to-surface ranging, and blind letdown modes) tied into the advanced SNAR navigation system (Uliss 47 INS and Dassault Electronique M 182 digital central computer) with data displayed on the HUD. The reconnaissance suite's internal components include the SAT Super Cyclope WCM 2400 IR linescanner in place of the starboard cannon, and an Omera 33 vertical or Omera 40 panoramic camera in a lower-nose bay. The type can also carry items such as the Thomson-CSF Raphaël TH SLAR pod, or Thomson-CSF ASTAC Elint pod for the detection of ground-based radars, or Dassault/Omera Harold long-range reconnaissance pod with an Omera 38 oblique camera, or Dassault/Omera COR-2 multi-purpose reconnaissance pod with visual and IR linescan sensors, or Dassault Nora or Thomson-CSF TMV-018 Syrel real-time optronic reconnaissance pod with video camera; SARA data-link equipment is standard for the real-time relay of information. A retrofit programme has added Matra Corail conformal chaff/flare dispensers under each wing root to complement the original fit of one Phimat chaff dispenser (to be replaced by the Matra Sycamor chaff/flare dispenser) and one Thomson-CSF Remora, Thomson-CSF Barem, Thomson-CSF Remora or Dassault Electronique Barrax single- or twin-band jammer pod.